Carcassonne
History and Architecture

Jean-Pierre Panouillé

A Gallic Oppidum, a landmark Roman town on the great route that linked the Mediterranean to the Atlantic, the strategic lock the Francs and Visigoths disputed themselves, a prosperous medieval City, the Cathar centre whose fall prepared the annexation of the Languedoc to the Capetian domain, a royal fortified town that remained, for nearly three hundred years, the guarantor of the Franco-Spanish peace, a great textile production centre at the end of the Ancien Regime, a decisive witness for the 19th-century rediscovery of the Middle Ages, nowadays a small regional capital and major City for tourism, Carcassonne was many a time at the very centre of History. Now registered by the UNESCO in their list of humanity's world heritage, along with the canal du Midi that flows along the lower town limits, the City is of course the essential centre of attraction. The larger part of this book is dedicated to it, and mainly focuses on the medieval period by analysing the architecture of the defences and relating the main sieges, but also by attempting to approach the inhabitants of Carcassonne's everyday life. The readers will however discover that Carcassonne is not only a medieval City, but also a town whose prehistoric and Roman pasts, similarly to its' evolution to the modern epoch, equally deserve to be remembered.

Translation: Fabe
Photographs: Catherine Bibollet

Editions Ouest-France

The City's towers are as many observatories from which one may discover very different landscapes. To the north, the heavy shapes of the Montagne Noire and its' sombre cover of forests announce the Massif Central. To the south, the Corbieres and the first Pyrenean crests obstruct the horizon. Delimited by these two mountainous masses, the narrow corridor that Carcassonne controls is the link between the Mediterranean and Oceanic worlds. To the west, prairies, wheat, barley, corn, and recently sunflower fields lead to the Lauragais, the "Gate of Aquitaine". To the east, one enters the Mediterranean Midi: the omnipresence of vine and the aridity of the garrigue testify to this.

Wind, as it engulfs itself into what geographers often name the "Carcassonne corridor" between the Massif central and the Pyreneans, is also a permanent feature of the Carcassonne climate. From the Mediterranean blows the Marin, also called the "vent d'autan" - a strong, hot, southerly wind. The greasy, humid and sticky Marin, the grey Marin which brings sadly mild, cloudy weather, or the black, violent Marin, carrier of heavy clouds that pour down in streams of rain. From the north comes the Cers; fresh, clear and vivifying wind, sometimes maybe even a little biting. As to the

The western and southern fronts.

The southern front, from the Grand Burlas tower to the Vade tower.

westerly winds, they bring fine and persistent rains from the Ocean. The river Aude, whose meander is overlooked by the City, leaves the south-north course it follows since it's Pyrenean spring, and inflects its' course towards the east, to reach the Mediterranean.

The actual town of Carcassonne stretches over an alluvial terrace built by the river. The City occupies the end of a small plateau, whose relief is fairly abrupt on the Aude side (the difference in altitude is approximately of 150 metres), and which gently slopes down towards the east.

Sandstone often shows on the surface below the high walls; it is this rock that has been used to construct the walls and towers, and it carries the scholar name of Carcassonne molasse; it was extracted either from the plateau itself, or from the surrounding hills.

The northern part of the City, from the counts' castle, to the west, to the Narbonnaise gate, to the east.

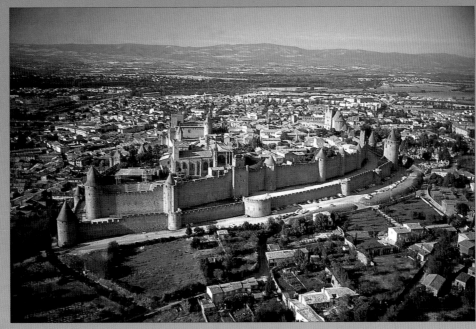

The southern front. In the background to the north, the Montagne Noire.

AERIAL VIEWS OF CARCASSONNE

Photos by Miegeville.

The City hill.
The very abrupt western flank
(towards the river Aude).
The gently sloping southern flank.

An oppidum on the great terrestrial road towards the Atlantic and Mediterranean

Approximately 2,5 km to the south-west of the City, the Carsac plateau welcomed, between the 8th and 6th centuries BC, what may be considered as the first Carcassonne town. A population of farmers, cattle breeders and hunters had begun forming a town in its' early stages, that was protected by a ditch to the east. Its' extent, the presence of fragments of Etruscan, Greek or Carthaginian ceramics allow us to think that Carsac was more than just a large village, and probably played the role of a trading centre between local resources and products from the Mediterranean world. Towards the middle of the 6th century, the Carsac site seemed to be abandoned in favour of the City.

Huts made of cane plaiting or adobe, silos buried in the ground intended to store provisions, a few traditional installations, a potter's furnace for instance, enclosures for animals then occupied the summit of the plateau that overlooks the Aude river. These still rather mediocre constructions, of which archaeologists could unearth a few remains, constituted an oppidum, i.e. a village perched on the heights, that may have been protected by a dry stone wall.

Approximately at the same epoch, throughout the whole of the Gaul Midi, similar towns were being constructed, perched at the summit of hills. For the populations of these oppidums, the aim was not only to better guarantee their own safety, but also to survey the passing of foreign merchants, and derive some benefits from them. For the Phoceans of Marseille, Agde or Ampurias were constant-

The western defences of the counts' castle, built on the part of the hill that the relief best protects.

Gallic vase turned on the lathe, 2nd century BC., Carcassonne City. Photo A. Guey.

ly venturing in greater numbers towards the inland. Placed as it was on the intersection of the major roads, the Carcassonne site was particularly well-visited.

Towards the south, the high-walled Aude valley and the Pyrenean passes lead to Catalonia; in the opposite direction, the footpaths of the Montagne Noire grant access to the regions of the Massif central. But above all, the City overlooks the great east-west road that, as it passes by the Narouze sill and the Carcassonne corridor, represents the shortest terrestrial passage between the Atlantic and the Mediterranean seas.

This was one of the pewter routes, a metal that was necessary to produce bronze, and that the elders went to collect in Cornwall. In the opposite direction, the Greek, Etruscan or Carthaginian productions were transported to Toulouse and the oceanic world. Some were offered to the first inhabitants of Carcassonne, as the amphora debris and fragments of ceramic found in the City's ground demonstrate. These commercial currents must have guaranteed the Carcassonne oppidum a certain level of prosperity that the actual excavations, performed in difficult conditions on rather outlying posts, can't really give an account of.

Recipient pierced with holes to drain cheese, 7th century BC., Carsac. Photo A. Guey.

The Tectosages: "Humble and simple people" in spite of their gold

Riding from central Europe around 300 BC., the Tectosage Volcae submitted the Iberians of the Languedoc. Relatively few in count, they embodied a military aristocracy which took control of the villages on the heights and fortified them, or at least improved their defences.

"Humble and simple people in their life", the Tectosages, according to the Greek geographer Strabon, whose works are dated from the very first years of our era, feared their gods, and gathered for them enormous quantities of gold and silver, in the shape of ingots and jewels.

Did those of Carcassonne, similarly to those of Toulouse, possess a fabulous trea-

Silver coin attributed to the Tectosage Volcae, 1st century BC., depot of Caunette-sur-Lauquet. Photo A. Guey.

The northern front. In the foreground, the outer walls and the Notre-Dame barbican which protects the City's northern entry (nowadays, the inner walls).

Western front, the Four-Saint-Nazaire tower (late Roman Empire tower), in the middle distance, the Inquisition tower (late 8th century).

FORTIFICATIONS

The eastern face of the counts' castle, turned towards the town. From left to right, the Saint-Paul tower, the castle entry, protected by two twin towers, the curtain, and the barracks' tower, crowned with hoarding (reconstitution).

The traverse of the Four-Saint-Nazaire tower at the level of the parapet. At the back, the stairs leading to the Inquisition tower.

In the foreground: the access ramp to the Aude gate (western City-gate).
The door is surmounted by a gatehouse and the curtain is sealed by a gallery (the Inquisition gallery) which leads
to the Justice tower. In the background, the counts' castle, whose defences, to the west, merge with the City's.

sure? This is likely, "the ground they possess abounds in gold", Strabon probably exaggerated a little, but he did not lie. The archaeologists proved that in the 2nd century BC., the precious metal was extracted from the depths of the Montagne Noire, as it still is nowadays in Salsigne. In some galleries dug at this epoch and located less than twenty kilometres to the north of Carcassonne, some miners' oil lamps have even been retrieved.

In spite of their gold, the Tectosages "ruled all luxury out of their lives", grew cereals whose grains they moulded, first using come-and-go millstones, then rotating ones; they bred goats, sheep, pigs, hunted for deer, boars and the smaller game that the Corbieres copse teemed with.

They also proved to be gifted craftsmen. The hand-shaped ceramics with rather grossly engraved decors gave way to earthenware turned on the lathe, whose paste was finer, and whose decors were more finely traced.

A small Gallo-Roman town
on the wine route

In 122 BC., consul Domitius Ahenobarbus travelled the Provence and the Languedoc as a conqueror. The elephant on which he liked to show himself and the discipline of his troops deeply impressed the populations. Rome's distant authority was fairly easily accepted, and sanctioned, more than it preceded, the Italian merchants' grip on the important market that the Gallic south embodied.

A Roman road was soon to pass at the foot of the *Carcasso* oppidum, linking Narbonne and Toulouse. It very rapidly became the great route of wine, a beverage which the Gauls had a strong liking for, and that the owners of the great domains in southern Italy transported to the Narbonne port in shiploads. A text written by Cicero draws a list of the toll booths that punctuated this road at the time of the governor Fonteius. Despite it's misspelled name, one of the stated towns does seem to be *Carcasso*. There, merchants had to pay a tax that represented approximately 50 % of the value of each amphora of wine they carried. As to the inhabitants of Carcassonne, they too drunk Italian wine, as fragments of Campanian amphorae discovered in the City prove, but they probably increasingly preferred local vintages to it. The culture of vine became generalised shortly before our era.

Located too close to Narbonne (the capital of the province) to become a major administrative and economic centre, Carcassonne remained a medium-sized town after the whole of Gaul was conquered by Caesar.

The town was probably elevated to the rank of a colony at the beginning of our era (*colonia Julia Carcasso*) and Pliny the Ancient lists it under the *oppida latina*. These words' meaning of "fortified town" makes no doubt, although we do not precisely know what kind of fortification this may have been. Under the Roman influence, habitations became more comfortable, the ground was covered with a pavement, walls were covered with a stucco coating, flat tiles with an edge (*tegulae*) and gutter tiles to connect them (*imbrices*) replaced the thatch and branch covers. Several visible rooms of a house in the castle court are decorated with a mosaic, whose simple decorative effects testify to a certain level of luxury.

The name of only one inhabitant of Carcassonne has reached us, that of a simple legionary: Caius Julius Niger, who died at the age of 45 after seventeen years of service, on the banks of the Rhine, in Mainz, where the second legion had led him, towards the middle of the first century AD.

Facing the brigands and the barbarians, the late Roman Empire walls

In the 8th century, the defence of the European frontiers, that the brave Caius Julius had peacefully ensured one hundred and fifty years earlier, gave way under the pressure exerted by the Germans. To the destruction caused by barbarians, who at this time sooner thought of pillage than of conquest, succeeded the danger caused by the "Bagaudes" - gangs composed of deserting soldiers, small landowners and town workmen who had lost all their money due to the destruction (or to the inflation, that was beyond the emperors' control).

The City's main entry (eastern entry). The pseudo-drawbridge that steps over the moat is a questionable restoration. The two projecting, spire-shaped towers of the Narbonnaise gate are typical of the very end of the 8th century.

To guarantee their own safety, the inhabitants of a large number of Gallic cities began to construct fortified enclosures. In 333, the itinerary of a pilgrim walking from Bordeaux to Jerusalem referred to Carcassonne as a castellum, i.e. a fortified town. Some elements of the actual inner walls, typical of the late Roman Empire's military architecture, are probably the remains of this fortification. Relatively shallow (1 to 2 metres), the Gallo-Roman foundations are composed of two or three layers of large stone blocks (maybe the re-use of a previous wall) that are often completed by a thick layer of extremely solid mortar. The walls are two to three metres wide. The small masonry facing (small-sized stones) is frequently interrupted by brick wall ties, whose purpose was certainly to correct the level and guarantee the enhance the final structure's solidity. Between the faced sides, some rubble, made of mortar in which stones, gravel or broken tiles had been embedded, gave the construction most of its' thickness. The mortar was obtained by mixing approximately one third of lime with two thirds of sand, to which one often added crushed bricks. Its' legendary solidity was probably due to the correct cooking degree of the lime and the methodical tamping down of the construction, to avoid any air bubbles. A rampart walk sheltered by a crenelated parapet probably overlooked the ground by approximately 8 metres, but further reconstructions in the Middle Ages never left these higher parts untouched.

To "reach the enemy's flank as he attacks the walls", as the Roman Vegece recommended, towers, that were flat on the City-side where there was no danger, were built in a semi-circular shape that projected towards the countryside. This shape guaranteed good resistance to battering ram assaults, and enabled multiple defensive firing angles. The lower part was full and served the purpose of a buttress for the walls. On the first floor, three semi-circular windows underscored by brick arches opened towards the countryside, which enabled the defenders to throw pilums, the Romans favorite weapon (a sort of large javelin) or handle slings. The upper floor, which rested on floorboards, was defended by battlements that supported a slightly sloping roof (tiles would not remain fixed on steeper roof structures).

The Romans were not very familiar with the longbow, this is why no arrow loops were to be found. As the efficiency of throwing weapons was limited, the distance between the towers did not exceed 30 metres. Defence therefore relied on two principles: firstly, to have the assaults break up on the thickness and solidity of the walls, and secondly, to inflict great losses on the enemy with the vertical firing from the top of the walls and towers.

The Gallo-Roman enclosure's layout, that is simply consolidated on the northern front, replaced to the south by a more modern fortification, and which at times merges with these fortifications to the east and west, often blends with the layout of the present-day inner walls. It only parts ways with it at the levels of the Moulin du Connetable tower and the Narbonnaise gate, where one may behold it, as it is slightly set back from the impressive medieval constructions.

With a perimeter of approximately one kilometre, the late Roman Empire walls enshroud a town whose surface slightly exceeds 7 hectares. Its' dimensions and appearance are somewhat reminiscent of the walls of Le Mans or Senlis, that were built at the same epoch, at the end of the 3rd century or the very beginning of the 4th century. Were these walls and towers of any use when facing the great invasions at the end of the 4th century and the beginning of the 5th century? They at least did avoid pillage and massacres, and helped negotiate an honourable surrender with the barbarians.

The Francs against the Visigoths, the Saracens facing Charlemagne, the times of legends

Riding from the regions of the Danube, the Visigoths, after roaming through Italy, conquered Spain and the Languedoc in the 5th century. It is in Carcassonne, according to Grégoire de Tours, that they hid their treasure, the fruit of Alaric's pillage of Rome, from the Francs' covetousness. "The admirable chandeliers of Salomon, king of the Hebrews, the vases adorned with precious gems that the Romans had once taken from Jerusalem" and many other riches may have been concealed at the bottom of the City's great well. This is what some inhabitants of Carcassonne still believed at the beginning of the 19th century, when they founded an association whose purpose was admittedly to dry out the great well, and retrieve the fabulous treasure.

The town's strategic importance, at the limit of the Franc and Visigoth kingdoms, gave the first historians the opportunity to discover what they thought to be a Visigothic construction, made of small masonry and brick wall ties, inside the City walls. Archaeology however clearly favours a late Roman Empire fortification. But nothing prevents us from thinking that the Visigoths may have performed a few reconstructions, that would for instance explain the brick foundations' irregular frequency. The town however undoubtedly did play the role of a fortified town, and was the lock which cut off the Frankish expansion towards the Mediterranean.

In 508, Clovis first tasted defeat. In 584, king Gontran, who did not accept the fact that "the frontiers of these horrible Goths extended themselves so far inside Gaul", led his best soldiers in a march against Carcassonne. But "the City's advantageous situation enabled it to oppose durable resistance".

In the beginning of the 7th century, Carcassonne this time had to repel the assaults of the Saracens. In the spring of 725, the Muslim governor of Spain, Anbasa Ibn Suhaym al Kalbi, who was simply named Ambisa by chroniclers, besieged the town, took hold of large spoils of war, and enslaved part of the population. The City then had to welcome an Arabian military contingent, and became Karkashuna. But in 759, under the impulse of Pepin the Short, the Arabs were driven out of Septimanie, and were repelled beyond the Pyreneans.

In the foreground, the outer walls and the Bérard tower. In the background, the imposing, massive shape of the Trésau tower.

The legend of the etymology of "Carcassonne"

The short-lived Saracen occupation inspired medieval writers some colourful legends, of which Charlemagne was of course the hero. The emperor was laying siege to the town held by Dame Carcas, a Muslim princess. Time passed, all that was left to feed the town's population was a small pig and a measure of wheat.

A believer in the efficiency of psychological war, Dame Carcas fattened the piglet up using the last ration of wheat, and threw the sated and plump animal over the walls. The emperor then gave up the idea of further besieging a town in which food was so abundant, that it was used to scoff at the enemy. As Charlemagne was moving away at the head of his troops, Dame Carcas had the trumpet sound (to sound = "sonner", Carcas sonne), and offered the returned emperor a truce.

When not used to justify etymology, the great emperor's legendary chanson de geste was used as the explanation for some architectural curiosities: "God, to show his power, made one of the towers lean before Charlemagne, as one may still see it today (the Vieulas tower), and let him take the town."

6th century BC.:
The early remains of habitats on the hills' summit. The birth of the **Carcasso** *oppidum, which controlled the great terrestrial road between the Atlantic and the Mediterranean. At the same epoch, not far away, where the motorway's rest area now is located, the large site of the Carsac plain (700 BC.) seems to have been abandoned.*

Original drawing by Gérard Guillier.

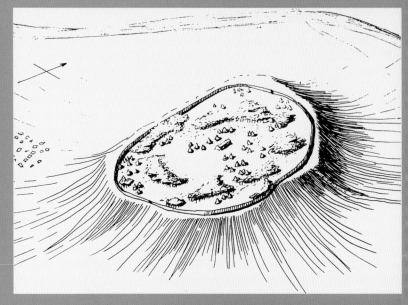

THE EVOLUTION OF THE CITY

4TH - 5TH CENTURY:
Succeeding to the long-lived Roman peace, a climate of insecurity settled in for a long time with the arrival of the barbarians. Towns surrounded themselves with thick walls. Gallo-Romans, and then Visigoths sheltered behind fortified walls, of which many elements still remain nowadays.   Original drawing by Gérard Guillier.

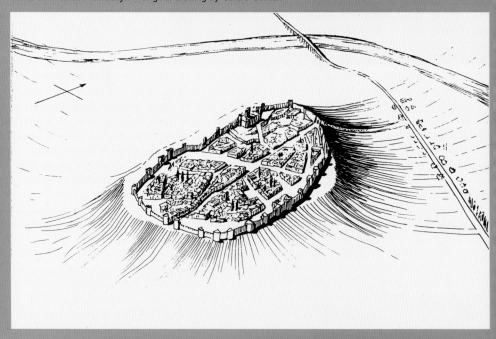

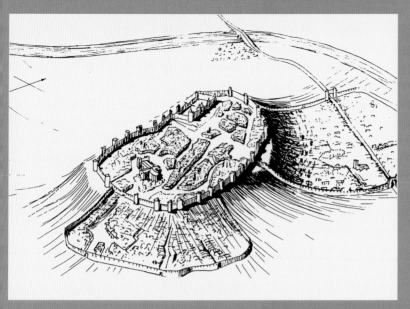

12TH CENTURY:
Demographic expansion and economic prosperity. The town stretches, far beyond it's walls, down the slopes of the hill. The two villages, Saint-Michel and Saint-Vincent, are built next to the old City.

Original drawing by Gérard Guillier.

SINCE THE 13TH CENTURY:
A fortified town in a country annexed to the Capetian domain after the Albigensian crusade, the guardian of the Franco-Spanish frontier, the City, by the will of the kings of France Louis IX and Philippe III, became one of the finest examples of medieval fortifications. The villages, which were a problem for active defence, were razed to the ground. On the other side of the Aude, the new town was founded, which gathered most of the commercial and handicraft activities. Original drawing by Gérard Guillier.

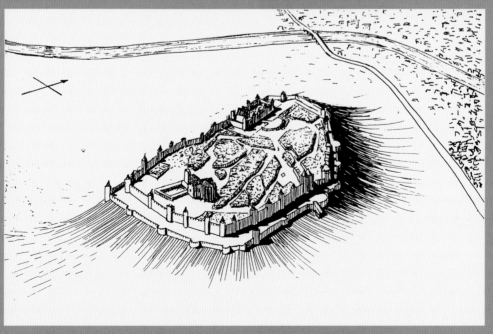

SKILFUL AND POWERFUL FEUDAL LORDS: THE TRENCAVEL

All began with a usurpation. In 1082, Bernard Aton Trencavel, viscount of Albi, Nîmes and Béziers, proclaimed himself viscount of Carcassonne. Related, by his mother, to the ancient dynasty, which had died out without any direct lineage, Bernard Aton was however not its' legitimate inheritor. But, torn apart as it was by family conflicts, the Barcelone house, which paid a fortune to buy the succession rights for Carcasses and Razes, was in no fit state to react. After two serious conflicts with his subjects, Bernard Aton definitively imposed his authority. Forty minor lords of the *castra* (fortified villages or castles), who had begun a rebellion in 1120, were dispossessed of their fiefs. Their wealth was used to reward the trustworthy men who had become the viscounts' new vassals. From there on, the Trencavel were to be, for nearly a century, solidly installed in Carcassonne. Their power, that was barely weakened by a few inheritance sharing-outs, was only inferior to that of the two great rival houses that were seeking control over the Midi: Toulouse and Barcelona.

After the marital union of the county of Barcelona and the kingdom of Aragon, king Alphonse II reigned supreme over the Pyrenean regions; his successors would later attempt to extend their influence over the whole of the Languedoc, until the Provence.

The count of Toulouse, Raymond de Saint-Gilles' feats during the first crusade helped reinforce the prestige of his lineage. The importance of their domain easily suggests that the counts of Toulouse were at the head of a large southern state.

Playing on the complexity of the federal relationships that bound them to their two powerful neighbours, and equally playing on the rivalry that opposed them, the Trencavel did not hesitate before requesting military support from Toulouse whenever their authority was questioned in Barcelona, nor did they fail to settle truces with the king of Aragon whenever they were in conflict with the counts of Toulouse. Very skilful when it came to reaffirming their domination on their lands, the Trencavel, according to a charter dated 1191, were the suzerains of a good sixty knights, and only for the viscounties of Béziers and Carcassonne. This therefore represented only a fraction of the faithful servants they could rely on; but it was already a force to be reckoned with, even at the scale of a kingdom.

In Carcassonne, the City was divided in sixteen "châtellenies" [boroughs]. A section of the walls, that usually included one or two towers, was placed under the responsibility of a trustworthy nobleman. He, his family and servants were requested to live in a house of the City, thus was this called the "service de l'estage" ["ester", in the ancient French language, meant "to reside"]. As a counterpart for this guarding service, the lord was granted a fief outside the City, as well as various privileges.

The castle at the time of the troubadours

As all great feudal lords of their times, the Trencavel loved adventures and great rides. Bernard Aton took part in the first crusade, and stayed in Palestine for four years; in 1118, "to fulfil a vow", he went to battle with the Moors on Spanish ground. His feats of arms were probably the inspiration for the mural which adorns one of the castles' rooms, the sole testimony of this medieval constructions' decoration that remains visible. It is in this room, "that was dubbed the round chamber, although it is rectangular, by the

Man playing the flute and child juggling with balls.
A court scene as one probably could see some playing
in the castle at the times of the Trencavel.
National Library, Paris.

castles' regular visitors", that the Trencavel settled their affairs. They received their vassals' homage "in the large room", or more often "under the elm tree, in the palace court".

Most of the buildings were built against the Gallo-Roman walls, and were flanked to the north by a now destroyed chapel, and to the south by a watchtower. Perpendicular to this alignment, a vast room defined a right-angled plane with the ensemble of habitable parts. The buildings that are visible nowadays have been, in some cases, heightened. The former flagstone covering (thick slabs of shale) and the course of the crenelated parapet that overlooked it appear fairly neatly at mid-height on the present façades. Large bays have now mostly replaced the narrow slits that once let a little daylight in.

Subsequently very deeply reconstructed, the inside of the "Palatium" is no longer reminiscent of feudal life, and the function of the various rooms is almost unknown to us. One may, most of the time, imagine walls coated with a form of paint, floors that were tiled or paved, and scarce furniture: coffers, tables, benches. Luxury was however not absent. A charter dated 1150 alludes to "the viscount's rich wardrobe, his gold and silver jewels, the vases, beds, rugs, hangings, tablecloths and all other such possessions…".

Troubadours and minstrels frequently stayed at the castle. Ramon de Miraval told his juggler: "Settle yourself in the Carcasses… I couldn't give you the names of all the barons who live there… for in such a courtly crowd, it is hard to make one's choice." Pierre Vidal admitted feeling "a complete joy when in the company of the dames of the Carcasses, whose behaviour and conduct pleased him greatly, as did those of the knights and barons and great-vassals of this country".

The bride of Roger II, (viscount from 1167 to 1194), Azalaïs or Adelaïde de Burlats, was paid the respects of Pons de la Garde, Guiraud de Salignac and Arnault de Maruelh. The latter told her about his dreams: "I close my eyes and sigh, and fall asleep sighing. Then my spirit flies straight to you, for the sight of whom it languishes. As I would desire to myself, night and day, every time I think about it, he courts you as he pleases, embraces you, kisses and caresses you…" But the unfortunate man was rejected, and supplanted by a high-ranking admirer, the king of Aragon himself.

Were all relations as perfectly platonic in these love courts -which were in fact kinds of courtly academies - where one debated subjects such as "can there be love between a husband and his wife"? René Nelli, one of the most eminent specialists in Occitan literature, is definitely not convinced this was the case.

This refined life, this cosmopolite entourage of Jewish savants, of Aquitan, Provencal or Spanish poets, this was all made possible thanks to the Trencavel's wealth. Their land returned important revenues, as did also a variety of seigniorial taxes and tolls they collected. For instance, they knew how to keep the monopoly of the salt sales to themselves, and the viscount's salt marshes, where the precious goods were stored, were a source of profit, as were the ovens, the mills or the press-houses which they owned.

The deniers, adorned on the obverse with the crescent, on the reverse with the crosier, and stamped to their name in the workshop nearby the Monnaie tower, appropriately symbolise the economic power these great feudal lords represented.

The inhabitants of Carcassonne's everyday life

The town was prosperous. Two fairs, one in spring, the other in autumn, attracted not only merchants from the Midi but also the Italian and Spanish merchants. One would find woollen cloths, skins and leathers of all sorts, knives, scissors for shearing sheep, and various metallic instruments. Cereals, wine, almonds, medicinal plants picked in the Corbières or on the Montagne Noire were brought for trading, as were many other products from the local farming or handiwork trades. During these high times of the urban life, people of course ate well. The food in Carcasses, in the 12th century, was abundant and fairly varied. Bread, the nutritional basis, was mostly made with wheat; it came in round loaves, flat loaves or brioches; a kind of waffle was also prepared, called the "oublie". Salt pork was the most frequently eaten meat, but the Carcassonne butchers also had beef on offer, for those who could afford it. Notaries and other men of law often received geese or capons as presents, and chicken stock was a dish of choice that was fed to the sick. The large number of fast days the Church ordered explains the importance fish had taken in that epoch's nutrition, be it sea or river fish: pike, raw salmon, salt mullet, hake, eel and trout were eaten daily. One fried fish, eggs, meatballs or simply breadcrumbs. The usual vegetables were cabbage, radish or turnips, beans, lentils, dry peas, onions, leeks. Food was cooked in an earthenware pot (*olla*), in cauldrons (*payrola*), in frying pans (*patella*), and people drunk abundantly. Meals were ended with goats' cheese, and various fruits: raisins, figs, apples, pears, quinces, cherries, strawberries, nuts… One of course drank wine, which was often watered down, and also a local wine called "brout". If the poor often were content with chestnuts, the rich had the opportunity to enjoy dates, ginger, cane sugar, figs with honey. At the beginning of the 13th century, a poor carpenter who worked on the construction of weaving looms earned 8 deniers per day. To justly celebrate the fair and forget about the daily cabbage and pork simmered in a pot, he could buy two eels (6 deniers) or a large fish pâté (5 deniers), and merrily spend the rest of his money in one of the town's taverns.

Eight days before the fairs began, for the whole duration of the transactions, and eight days after their closing, safety was ensured on the whole territory of the viscounty by detachments of men of arms in the pay of the Trencavel. In their own wisdom, or under popular pressure, they then put an end to the arbitrariness of their power. No exceptional contribution could be levied without the notables' assent. The inhabitants of Carcassonne could dispose of their wealth by will, and the taxes collected on the sales of salt, fish, wheat and meat were no longer on the lords' pleasure, but determined by a charter. Another written document, published under the name " Beneath the elm, before the Palace " governed, taking inspiration from the Roman right to direct the relationship between creditors and debtors: it described the functioning of the seigniorial justice. The supreme control over all that concerned the administration, justice and the levying of taxes belonged to a "viguier" [a provost], a kind of civil servant from the Palace, who was soon to be seconded by a "sub-viguier". Nonetheless, twelve men of experience and integrity, elected yearly, governed and administered their affairs, and those of the Carcassonne community, by defending the latter's rights, privileges and freedom before the viscounts' people.

The first floor of the counts' castle, western wing. The various rooms, countless times reconstructed, now shelter a lapidary store. To the centre, an ablution basin (12th century, from the Lagrasse or Fontfroide abbeys).

How many inhabitants were these notables, that were soon referred to as consuls, supposed to represent? In the absence of texts, one may estimate that the population living only in the shelter of the enclosure was certainly no greater than a few hundred people.

The City and its' villages in the 12th century, a rapidly-expanding urban ensemble

In the times of the Trencavel, two large villages surrounded the City. The eldest village seems to be the Saint-Michel market town, originally named Castellare, which occupied the south of the plateau. The present Citadins cemetery that one may see ahead of the Narbonnaise gate is only an extension of the cemetery that once was located alongside the Saint-Michel church, constructed "near the walls of Carcassonne". The Razès gate, located approximately at the place of the present Saint-Nazaire gate, established a direct link between this market town and the City. To the north, on the hill's slopes, was the market town of Saint-Vincent. The habitations were huddled around the church that carried the same name (and of which nothing now remains) and around the church of Sainte-Marie (the present Notre-Dame de l'Abbaye church). The City's north gate, also called the Bourg gate, led to this town. Both villages were surrounded with "walls, towers and ditches". The joining of the Saint-Vincent village walls with those of the City still remains visible nearby the Moulin d'Avar tower. Many gates, the Salin gate, the Amandiers gate... opened out towards the countryside or towards a more interspersed concentration of habitats, where houses alternated with vines, gardens, vegetable gardens or pastures ("farratjals", in the Occitan language). This is what was referred to as the "suburbium". Between the City and the Aude river for instance, numerous constructions tended to form another market town: Granoillant or Graveillant.

Around 1200, on the eve of the Albigensian crusade, churches, middle-class houses, modest buildings, garden sheds, workshops, craftsmen's stalls, warehouses for salt or wool were clinging to the slopes of the hill, that the City overlooked. The Aude water mills ensured the supplies of flour. There was no shortage for water, that of the river, but that too of Fontgrande in the Saint-Michel market town, or water from another spring that gushed forth nearby the Aude gate. The hillocks' sandstone was very permeable but a few veins of clay, at different levels in the soil, contributed to form pockets of water, that were true natural cisterns. It would be very surprising if, among the good twenty wells that the City still counts, none had been dug in more ancient times.

Carcassonne, for the pilgrim or for the 12th century merchant coming from the north, was less of a fortified town than a prosperous City on the road to Spain and the Mediterranean. After having passed over the Aude on the one and only wooden bridge at the time, the journeyman walked through rather rustic-looking boroughs, entered one of the two fortified market towns, climbed the populous and busy streets to reach the old Gallo-roman walls, of impressive thickness and solidity. Below, circling this urban ensemble that testified to the regions' economic vitality, the City, with the houses of the noble lords who guarded it, the viscounts' castle, the bishop's palace, the house and cloister of the canons, and the barely finished Saint-Nazaire cathedral.

First floor of the counts' castle:
in the foreground, arcades taken from a house
in the lower town (14th century).

On June 11th 1096, pope Urbain II blessed the stones that had been prepared for the building site of the Saint-Nazaire cathedral. The construction was completed by the first third of the 12th century. At the end of the 13th century, a transept and a gothic choir would replace the Roman chevet, of which all that remains is the crypt that supported it. Of the Roman cathedral now only remains the gothic cylindrical nave, shouldered by the semi-circular vaults of the two narrow side aisles. One entered by the north, at the level of the third bay, as one still does today. The gate's tympanum was maybe painted, as were the arches which rested on the small columns. The sculpted decor has been restored with a very relative exactitude; the battlements that surmount the western face, and suggest that the Roman cathedral was fortified, are an unfortunate 19th-century addition.

A few years after the cathedrals' construction, the Cathar contagion, "in the way of a chancre", gained the City.

The Cathars

The "fellows" or "the poor of Christ", as they called to call themselves, never claimed to have created a new religion, and always asserted drawing their faith from the Gospels. Catharism was however frequently depicted as an imported religion, born of the dualistic visions of the world that were developed in Persia by Zarathustra (8th century BC.), and then by Manes (2nd century AD). Still strongly preached in the Balkans by the Bogomils (the Bulgarians), Manichaeism (the doctrine of Manes) embodied a conception of the world in which the forces of good and evil opposed each other. It supposedly reached western Europe through the intermediary of the merchants, pilgrims or crusaders returning from the Holy land. These are possible influences. One may also see in this theological thinking and the return to primitive Christianism that spread themselves after the year one thousand, the origin of a movement that wished to remain faithful to the "true" faith.

The Cathars always referred themselves to the Gospels. But they selected some passages and interpreted them as they would have liked them to be.

Discoidal steles (12th-14th centuries). Frequently seen in the Lauragais and Pyrenean regions, they marked the location of a tomb. No connection has been confirmed between this shape and Catharism. The stele in the foreground depicts the paschal lamb, the emblem of the lower town.

The God of goodness and love announced by Christ could never have been implied with a world of misery, cruelty and lies. God reigned in another, invisible world. The material world was the work of Satan, and Christ only took human appearance to remind men of the existence of the real God, and to draw them back to the Father. Negating incarnation, they refused all materiality in the sacraments, to only retain the "consolamentum", the purification by the laying on of the hands, that made the believer a "perfect" being.

Leading an ascetic life, aspiring to rid themselves of their mortal coil, asserting that all souls were good and that all would be saved, the "fellows" preached a form of Christianism that was very distant from the official Church's teachings. They reject all images, all symbols, including the cross, all reference to God in the explanation of natural phenomena; no event in this world was due to divine will, no authority could claim itself of God. Gathered as a "counter-Church", living in exemplary simplicity and honesty, bringing simple answers to fundamental anguishes (Evil, Salvation...), the Cathars were a threat to the complex construction of the catholic dogma, and sapped the authority of a clergy that was engaged in a world that they thought to be a mere ephemeral hell.

Under various names (the Patarins in Italy, the Pifles in Flanders), the Cathars were present almost everywhere throughout Europe. However, only the Languedoc saw this heresy take root and comfort its' first successes. The mediocrity of part of the local clergy played in favour of their new ideas. The archbishop of Narbonne, Bérenger, "knew no God other than money, and had a purse in the place of his heart", admitted pope Innocent III. The indifference of the population also gave Catharism the chance to develop. The bishop of Carcassonne so terribly bored the towns' middle class by continuously denouncing the Cathar danger, that no-one would talk any longer with this "bore". The Carcassonne heretics could therefore name, in 1167, the "perfect" Guiraud Mercier, and organise a Church that rivalled with Rome, all in broad daylight. The feudal lords were actually delighted to see the clergy questioned, since the Gregorian reform had seen this clergy escape from their grip and become reluctant to pay them the tithes and other ecclesiastic benefits which they had taken over. Those of the Trencavel's surroundings granted the "fellows" right of sanctuary and lent an obliging ear to their views, when they were not simply converted to Catharism! Guilhem Peyre de Brens, seneschal of the Trencavel for the Albigensian region, refused to be buried in Christian ground, and asked to be laid to rest among the "fellows". Bertrand de Saissac, Roger II of Trencavel's best friend, his son's tutor, gave the monks of the Alet a rough ride and passed himself as an expert in the Catharic doctrine. Roger II himself, viscount from 1167 to 1194, was excommunicated for a while, so brutal and unscrupulous was his conduct towards the Church. His son Raymond Roger seemed to have been raised in catholic faith. Out of tolerance, or liking for oratory jousts, he however enabled the Cathar bishop of Carcassonne, Bertrand de Cimorre, and eleven of his people to be confronted in a "colloquium" to twelve representatives of the catholic Church, among which Brother Raoul and Pierre de Castelnau, the pope's legate. The whole court attended the "debates", which were chaired by the king of Aragon himself as he was passing in the City (1204). Declared heretics by the sovereign, but recognised as worthy of being listened to, the "fellows" would continue to freely expose their doctrine. Did Pierre Roger de Cabaret, one of the viscounts' closest counsellors, not warmly welcome them to his castles in Lastours?

How many heretics were there in the City and its' boroughs? One cannot tell. To establish a comparison, one may recall that in Béziers, when the crusaders entered the town, the list of the Cathars and sympathisers made out by the bishop comprised some 220 names. An identical number is plausible for Carcassonne.

The Cathars were probably always a minority group among the population. But even though the heresy was not ignored by the poor people and did make some converts among them, it was proportionally more widespread among the elite: lords, chatelaines, women of high condition, seigniorial officers, men of law, merchants, rich craftsmen… The example given by the members of the more prominent social levels and the constitution of a true parallel Church particularly worried the catholic clergy.

The crusade: the 1209 siege, the surrender

The murder of legate Pierre de Castelnau, on January 14th 1208, unleashed the anger of pope Innocent III against Raymond VI de Toulouse. The pope summoned a crusade. Sensing danger, Raymond VI submitted himself and made amends; better still, he also accepted the Cross. So, who was to be punished, who could be castigated? *The crusade's hymn* provided the answer: "They thought they would take Toulouse, but she made her peace. They will take, they say, Carcassonne and the Albigensian region."

Raymond Roger Trencavel was 24 years old, was a catholic, but the heresy infected his lands; the young viscount would pay for the expedition.

In Béziers, a false manoeuvre on behalf of the defenders enabled the rovers to enter the town. They were given over to a frightful massacre. The town was no more than a mass of blackened ruins when, on July 26th 1209, the army of the crusaders walked on Carcassonne. There, the viscount had gathered as many knights as he could. To complete and consolidate the fortifications, one did not hesitate to demolish the refectory, the canons' storeroom in the cathedral and even the church's stalls, in order to reclaim the materials.

The siege began on August 1st. Raymond Roger, with all the impatience typical of his youth, suggested they immediately attempted a sortie, but Pierre Roger de Cabaret persuaded him not to waste his forces. On the third day, the crusaders took control of one of the boroughs, the less fortified one. For the follow-up of the events, let us hear the tale of Pierre des Vaux de Cernay, who was the nephew of one of the clergymen, and was leading the crusade: "On the next day, our troops headed for the walls of the second town and launched an attack on it: the viscount and his people defended themselves with such courage that our troops had to evacuate the ditch they had entered, because of the frequent and heavy rains of stones. In this fight, it happened that one of our knights, his thigh broken, lay in the ditch; no-one dared to help him get out because of the ceaseless rain of stones, but one brave man, the count of Montfort, jumped into the ditch, accompanied by one single horseman, and saved the wounded man at the peril of his own life. When this was done, the crusaders soon unlimbered machines called balistas (a kind of catapult) in order to demolish the walls around the borough. Once the balistas had caused some damage at the top of the walls, the crusaders brought, with great difficulty, a four-wheeled cart to the foot of the walls, that was covered with a cow's skin, under the shelter of which specialists were to sap the ramparts. This cart was soon destroyed by the enemy, who was unceasingly throwing fire, wood, and stones, but the sappers found refuge in the niche they had already dug, so that their work did not run late. At the break of day, the sapped wall fell down and our troops entered by the breach with a great din. The enemies first retreated to the higher parts of the City, but as they saw our knights retreat from the town and return to their tents, they came out of the town, giving chase to the men who had stayed behind, killing those who could not leave, setting fire to the whole town, and then retreated back to the heights."

This way, in a few days' fighting, both boroughs had been destroyed. But the City, with its' solid walls, had not yet undergone an assault. Each camp were counting their dead. The crusaders feared a long siege that would be costly in men, and more than anything wanted to take the town intact - so far, the losses had been too high; what point was there in being the ruler of a few charred ruins? In the City, the situation was critical. Women, children, farmers of the surroundings and inhabitants of the boroughs were surviving, on top of each other, in appalling hygienic conditions. It was the month of August, the inhabitants of Carcassonne no longer had access to the Aude river, nor to the fountains of the boroughs. Would the City's wells suffice to supply a plethoric population? Besides, no exterior help should be expected. And finally, the horrible massacre of the population of Béziers was haunting everybody's minds. It was therefore in both side's interest to negotiate. What was said? What happened exactly? Texts remain unclear or silent about this. On August 15th, all was over, Raymond Roger had turned himself in to the crusaders. But his sacrifice also saved the population: "The inhabitants of the town, and the knights who were also staying there, and also the dames and damsels, all, as always, left the town... Without taking anything with them, in great haste, they left, clothed only with their shirts and breeches; some fled to Toulouse, others to the provinces of Aragon or to Spain, some headed north, some headed south."

In the hope that the viscount's family would return, their treasure was buried in the castle court. Three "treasures" were recovered in the north-western angle of the court: some twenty deniers and oboles of Carcassonne that had been stamped under the reign of Raymond Roger, and a bit further on, a sandstone vase containing two kilograms of coins, Melgorian deniers; and finally, in the same area, coins agglomerated in piles of 20 to 30 copies. For some, then, the war was not yet over, Carcassonne was not definitely lost to the enemy. With the City vanquished, the crusaders however could consider themselves as the rulers of the country.

THE CATHARS

Fra Angelico: the miracle of fire (early 15th century). This painting is reminiscent of one of the episodes of Saint Dominique's life. Dressed in an austere way, he embraced the simple and exemplary life of the "fellows", and searched to draw populations who had been lead into Catharism back to the "true faith". According to the legend, the manuscript negating the Cathar theses, that he here hands to a rich townsman, would be thrown three times into the fire, but would always be taken out of it intact.

Louvre Museum. © RMN, photo H. Lewandowski.

Prisoners taken to be executed. Miniature of the customs of Toulouse, 1296, BN, ms. lat. 9187 fol. 33.

... Angelico, the miracle of fire.
... catholic theses are spared by the fire.
... may connect a very ancient medieval
...iciary practice with this episode: the ordeal,
...ich was condemned in 1215 by the council
...Latran; the accused was proved to be innocent
... a wound inflicted by fire healed rapidly.
...the 13th century, the church set up a modern
...ocedure: an inquiry, with an interrogation and
...rch for witnesses.
...this sense, the Inquisition was a step forward,
...n if its' excesses must be denounced.

...vre Museum. © RMN,
...to H. Lewandowski.

Pope Gregory IX gives the Dominicans
the mission to fight the Albigensian heresy.
Manuscript. Sainte-Genevieve Library, Paris.

Registers of the Inquisition.
Manuscript, dated 13th century.
Archives of the town of Toulouse.

Simon de Montfort, new viscount of Carcassonne

Under the pressure of the pope's legate, the City, all the wealth it contained and the Trencavel's lands were handed over to one of the crusade's most active lords: Simon de Montfort. A brave man (he fought for God and therefore feared nothing, it pleased him to say) and a fervent catholic who did not overburden himself with scruples (heretics are God's enemies, they must therefore be killed). On his lands of Montfort, in the Yvelines, in the Parisian region, (one did not yet talk about Montfort-l'Amaury), and during the fourth crusade, he more than demonstrated qualities of rectitude and energy, and also that he was a born leader, which did not go unnoticed by his friend, the prelate Gui des Vaux de Cernay. He was besides this a very good friend of Philippe Auguste, a man the king showed much appreciation for.

Raymond Roger Trencavel died in a cell on November 10th 1209, and his son Raymond was but a child whose safekeeping had been entrusted to the count of Foix before the disaster. The City became the headquarters for the troops leaving on expeditions against the rebellious lords and the heretic towns. In 1215, prince Louis, Philippe Auguste's elder son, spent the month of May in the City, accompanied by many lords of noble lineage. The Cathars were being hunted down. The inhabitants Carcassonne who were not suspected of being heretics had soon returned. They assisted to the unfortunate Trencavel's funeral, but also to the merrymaking for the baptism of Petronille, Simon's third daughter to be born in the City, and for the marriage of his elder son Amaury with Beatrix of Burgundy. Saint-Dominique presided over both ceremonies that took place in the Saint-Nazaire cathedral.

The seal of Viscount Raymond Roger Trencavel, dispossessed in 1209. Museum of Béziers.

Little by little, the boroughs were being rebuilt, and everyone displayed at least an appearent submission. It was known that all treason would immediately be repressed; the "French" lived in the fear of denunciations, murder attempts and ambushes. A cleric who had helped heretics out tied to a horse's tail, and dragged through all the City's streets, before being hanged. It was known and told that the inhabitants of Bram had had their noses cut off and their eyes burst, and that in Minerve, 140 "perfects" had been burnt at the stake. The "Pamiers Statutes", a legislation that was rather profitable to the City inhabitants and farmers that the count promulgated, did nothing to help forget this merciless battle against the heretics.

For eight years, Simon de Montfort, who was always on campaign, succeeded in keeping the country under his control, even if he didn't succeed in destroying all opposition. On June 25th 1218, as he was trying to reconquer Toulouse, Montfort died, struck by a projectile from a balista. His son Amaury did not succeed in standing up to the two powerful lords who then joined forces against him: Raymond VII of Toulouse and the count of Foix.

At the end of the year 1222, Amaury de Montfort, without a denier to his name, could rely on no-one else than his uncle Gui, Marshal Gui de Levis, and another few dozen knights. In desperate straits in his own town, he succeeded in negotiating his departure. On January 15th 1223, he left the City and rode towards his ancestors' land, in the Ile-de-France. The way was clear for the son of the man defeated in 1209. At the age of 17, this protégé of the counts of Foix proudly proclaimed himself in a charter, dated February 1224: "Trencavel by the grace of God, viscount of Béziers, of Carcassonne, of the Razes and of Albi". His joy was to be short-lived.

The annexation to the royal domain and the construction of the outer walls

In Paris, Amaury de Montfort handed his rights on the Languedoc over to king Louis VIII; as a counterpart, he hoped to receive the sword of a Constable. In the Carcasses, the Cathars were now recovering. The fellows, among which a certain Barthélémy de Carcassonne was to be found, preached in the castra of Montreal, Saissac and Montolieu. Houses of "perfects", replicas of catholic convents, were reported everywhere. On January 28th 1226, Raymond VII de Toulouse and his "accomplices", among which Raymond Trencavel, were excommunicated. A new crusade began, led by the king.

The people of Carcassonne, as most of their compatriots of Languedoc, were tired with war. As Louis VIII was still only in Avignon, a deputation of townsmen came to hand him the keys to the town. They were not the only ones to do this: those of Albi, Saint-Gilles, Beaucaire, Narbonne, Arles, Tarascon, Orange… also pleaded for royal leniency. Raymond Trencavel was forced to flee. The king empowered a Carcassonne seneschal, Eudes le Queux, and Maître Clairin, the former chancellor under Simon de Montfort, replaced bishop Bernard Raymond de Roquefort, who was deemed to be spineless when facing the heresy. Gui de Montfort, Simon's brother, Gui de Levis, Pierre de Voisins and other barons from the north recovered their fief.

In the years following the establishment of the seneschal's power in Carcassonne, works were carried out, destined to make the town able to defend itself. But in the absence of texts, it is now impossible to state any precise dates.

The Saint-Nazaire tower, southern gate; seen from the inside of the City. On the first floor, the lodge for the operation of one of the two portcullises.

It is likely that the fortified "curtain" that surrounds the viscount's housing on three sides has been built at this time. The towers' surbased dome vaults seem rather archaic. On the other hand, the rectangular plan, the entry placed between two twin towers and surmounted with two floors, each commanding a portcullis and machicolations, the stirrup-shape of the arrow-loops' bases, their disposition in staggered rows that multiplied the possible firing angles and reduced the walls' weakness, are all fairly representative of the progress made under the guidance of the royal architects since Philippe Auguste. This fortification, facing the town, says a lot about the way the French mistrusted the City's population during these first years of royal occupation.

Just as present in their minds, the fear of an attack from the outside made the protection offered by the ancient Gallo-Roman walls seem insufficient. These were therefore surrounded by a first line of defence that corresponds, with a few exceptions, to the present outer curtain. The walls, made of medium-sized masonry, were regularly interrupted by horseshoe-shaped towers that were "open at the throat", i.e. open towards the town, so the enemy who had taken them could not use them for shelter.

The existence of concentric walls had many advantages. It made it possible to oppose the enemy with two lines of archers, in echelons. It

*The western bailey
from the passage of the bishop's square tower.
In the background, the Cahuzac tower.*

of course made sapping more difficult, as two successive curtains needed to be demolished. And finally, it made room, between the two curtains, for an area where the assailant who had passed the first obstacle would necessarily find himself on unfavourable ground: exposed, with no possibilities of attempting a manoeuvre or an easy retreat, exposed to the fury of the cavalrymen who, when attempting a sortie, used this passage as a boulevard to liberate the immediate surroundings of the inner curtain.

The bailey, this is the name given to this space between the two walls, needed to be levelled, as the hills' relief often gave it a sloping profile which did not make things easy for eventual traffic. The earth was removed from the base of the Gallo-Roman walls and transferred a few metres downhill, in order to heighten the level of the

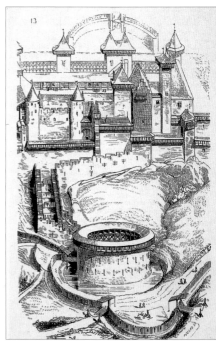

*The castle, and the Aude barbican.
Restitution. Drawing by Viollet-le-Duc ("Dictionary of Architecture"
and monograph on Carcassonne published in 1858).*

ground behind the outer curtain. This did not go easily. The foundations of the Roman walls and towers had been un-earthed, the foundations dated of the late Roman Empire needed to be reconstructed, and to a fairly considerable depth at that. A few sections of walls fell down, one tower leaned slightly to it's side, the tower next to it leaned dangerously and lost its' upper floor. Reconstructions and consolidations were performed, discharging arches were placed where neces-sary in order to better distribute weights. These deep moves, that are visible on the northern front, clearly demonstrate the will to attend the most urgent needs first, at a time when the French Midi was far from being pacified.

The curtains of the inner walls, the passage from the Inquisition gallery to the Justice tower.

The 1240 revolt, the royal garrison stands fast in the City

Raymond Trencavel was fretting in the province of Aragon where he had taken refuge. He dreamt of retrieving his lands. Many lords of the Corbières and Montagne Noire provinces were ready to heed to his call. In 1240, at the age of 33, he risked his all. Olivier de Termes, Jourdain de Saissac and all those who were exasperated by the royal authority and the Church's relentlessness towards the heretics met him in Roussillon.

In Carcassonne, seneschal Guillaume des Ormes organised his defence. Food and livestock were requisitioned, war machines were constructed. Messengers were sent to Bourges, where the king was staying, to ask him for help. The City's population was widely composed of "Frenchmen" or parti-sans of the king, but the population who returned to occupy and rebuild the boroughs that were de-stroyed in 1209 seemed far less trustworthy.

On September 7th, the bishop of Toulouse and the seneschal came to exhort the inhabitants of Saint-Vincent, who were gathered in the Sainte-Marie church. All swore upon the host, the relics and the holy Gospels that they would remain faithful to the king. And on the night that followed the next day, they handed the town over to Trencavel.

For one whole week, the rebels attempted no sortie against the City; with the population's help, they dug mining galleries, a veritable underground network which they intended to use to sap the curtains. Guillaume des Ormes explained: "They started their mines from the houses, so we knew nothing until they reached our bailey." On September 17th, a sortie led by the seneschal against the town of Graveillant was successful. But on the following days, Trencavel and his men took control of the river Aude's banks. An artillery duel opposed a "mangonnel" brought by Trencavel to a "Turkish balista" positioned by the "French". And on either side, crossbows, relatively new weapons at the time, were causing many victims.

Until the end of the month, the mining works were lead in at least five different places. They did not enable the decisive assault by the breaches they opened, as the concentric walls played their role well. Besides, the defen-ders had time to raise makeshift obstacles behind the sections which they suspected were going to fall.

Ladders

Murder holes

Hoarding

Arrow loops

Spur-shaped tower

"Chatte"

Bailey

Mantlet

Hoarding

Tower "open at the throat"

Scarp

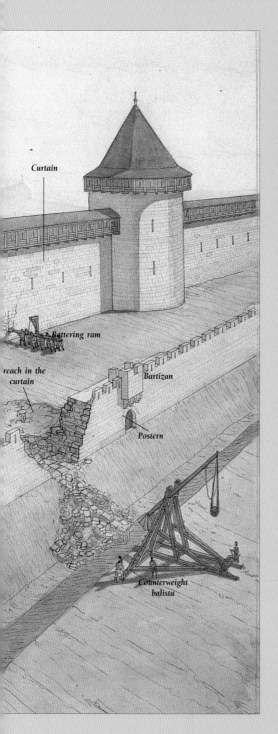

Curtain

Battering ram

reach in the
curtain

Bartizan

Postern

Counterweight
balista

Drawing by Jean-Claude Golvin © Géo, 1993.

THE ATTACK OF A CASTLE IN THE 12TH AND 13TH CENTURIES

Besides the attack that was launched using ladders, the method most frequently used to create a breach was sapping. Sheltered below wooden galleries called "vignes" or "chattes", the sappers reached the walls, pulled some of their stones free and dug a deep cavity, which they propped up as they progressed. When the wall section held up by the props was wide enough, they set fire to these structures and retreated. Deprived of their support, the wall section would come down. The same manoeuvre, using underground galleries, was called mining. The sappers, or any other enemy who had reached the walls, remained invisible to the defenders atop the parapets. They needed to lean far forward and therefore expose themselves, which is the reason why flankings were developed, that would enable the defenders to see and reach the assailant at the very base of the walls. The lateral flanking was ensured by the towers that, due to their projecting shape and to the arrow loops pierced on their flanks, enabled shots parallel to the wall. The vertical flanking was made possible by the construction of hoarding, overhanging wooden galleries that were equipped with trapdoors, and then by the same system made out of stone, called the machicolations. This last word originally characterised the slit or hole through which one could reach the attacker at a vertical angle. Beams were slipped in the "murder holes" dug in the battlement wall, when necessary, to support these galleries.

Two final means made the capture of a town possible. Starving the population required a lot of patience, large troops to control the whole perimeter of the walls and doors, and important logistics, for the assailants also needed to be supplied - and quite on the contrary of many generally accepted ideas concerning pillages, they most often bought their food from the local farmers. In the City, the number of wells and cisterns was greatly increased during the great works of the 12th century. Treason, finally, was often used. To prevent this, in case of a siege, the secondary doors were walled, and the main doors in Carcassonne were blocked by two portcullises, that were operated in two different places, and the responsibility of which was of course given to different teams.

The 1240 siege

(Excerpts from Guillaume des Ormes' report, seneschal of Carcassonne)

The siege stone (Saint-Nazaire basilisk)
Bas-relief of unknown origin, representing the siege of a town. Beginning of 12th century?
Photo J.-P. Bouchard.

"The City of Carcassonne is under siege by the one who claims to be the viscount and his accomplices... (a group) settled between the City's end and the river... they entrenched themselves so well that we could no longer reach them. Another detachment... established itself between the bridge and the castle's barbican... There were so many crossbowmen in these two positions that no-one could leave the City without being wounded. Then they raised a mangonnel in front of our barbican, and against this machine we raised a very good Turkish balista. Besides, Madame, they began to dig a mine against the barbican of the Narbonnaise gate, but as soon as we heard the miners at work, we counter-mined and built a dry stone wall in the barbican that was large and strong, so that a half of the barbican was well guarded. Then they lit a fire in the gallery they had dug, and once the props had burnt, part of the barbican came down... Please also know, Madame, that since the beginning of the siege, they were ceaselessly launching attacks against us. But we had great quantities of fine crossbows... On one Sunday, they gathered all their soldiers, the crossbowmen and the others, and all together launched an assault on the barbican under the castle, we went down to the barbican with so many stones and crossbow bolts, which we used to overcome them, that they retreated, with many dead or wounded... Then... they learnt that our people, Madame, were coming to help us; so they set fire to the houses in the borough... and all taking part in the siege retreated at night, stealthily, and those in the boroughs too. I must say, Madame, that by the grace of God,... in spite of their siege, even the poorest of us lacked no food. On the contrary, Madame, we had large quantities of wheat and meat... To finish, please know that they had started mining strongly in seven places, and that we counter-mined everywhere we could, without sparing ourselves. They started digging from their houses[1], so we could see nothing until they reached our bailey..."

1. The houses of the borough.

On September 30th, Trencavel attempted a general attack, that was a failure. On October 6th, a new attack was repelled. On the 11th, informed of the approach of the relief army that Louis IX had placed under the orders of Jean de Beaumont, his chamberlain, the viscount ordered a retreat. The inhabitants of the boroughs set fire to their houses, and fled with the small rebel army; they knew that the king's men made traitors pay harshly for their deeds.

Trencavel, once again sheltering in Spain, was only pardoned in 1247. He solemnly renounced to all his rights and took part in Saint Louis' first crusade. His good conduct in Egypt was rewarded by a few lands in the Corbières. There he remained until his death, with his two sons, who disappeared without any known lineage. In the same year 1247, the king forgave the borough's inhabitants and authorised them to come back. They did not even find the ruins of their houses, the seneschal had had everything razed to the ground.

Fight between Frankish knights and Saracens (detail), Mural adorning the springs of the "round chamber's" vault. The only room of the castle to have kept a fragment of its' medieval decor (late 12th century?). Photo by Miegeville.

The castle's eastern gate (town side) and the bridge, once crossed by a wooden footbridge that led over the ditch.

On the place of the borough of Saint-Michel was raised the mighty Vade tower, whose construction was finished in 1245. Built over a well, equipped with a baker's oven, it was composed of an ensemble of three ribbed vaults, surmounted by two levels on floorboards. Settled in the wall's thickness, an intriguing stairway followed the wall's curve; it lead to a parapet, from which the eye could see above the undulation of the borough of Saint-Michel. Very tall, circular, pierced with many arrow slits, the Vade tower presented itself as an independent defence element. The garrison could stand fast even if the outer curtain was lost, and the tower then was a threat to the back of the enemy who was launching an attack on the second curtain. The nearby Peyre tower seems to have been erected at the same epoch. At the foot of this one, in the ditch, a door gave access to an underground passage that led to the City, or made it possible to leave it discreetly. A well, accessible by this gallery, had been dug beneath the bailey. In all places, the damage incurred in 1240 had been repaired with great care. But the seneschal authorised no constructions in the City's immediate surroundings; he wanted to make sure that an eventual enemy could only advance on open ground.

The castle's western face. Its' fortifications here merge with the towns' walls. The Flemish gable is a questionable restoration.

*Reconstitution of a battering ram:
the assailants, in the shelter of this cart,
gave a pendular movement to a long
wooden bar that was suspended by chains,
and ended with a metallic hood (sometimes
in the shape of a ram's head). The aim was
to force the wooden doors open or to
weaken the masonry of the walls or towers.
The beak- or spur-shape of some 13th century towers made it possible to reinforce
its' central part against battering ram
assaults, and deflected the latter's blows.*
Photo Renaud Beffeyte

*Reconstitution of a belfry or assault tower.
Pushed forward against the walls and equipped with a
drawbridge, these towers enabled the assailants to set foot on
the parapet. The engineers who directed their construction
were required to estimate as closely as possible the height of
the walls. The moat, whether it was dry or not, prevented
these towers from approaching, unless it was filled by the
assailants.* Photo Renaud Beffeyte.

*Reconstitution of a throwing machine:
the shank's short part was composed of a chest filled
with earth that acted as a counterweight; to lower the
chest, one could use a wheel similar to those used on
medieval building sites to
raise loads.* Photo Renaud Beffeyte.

The castle hoarding's gallery. To the right, crenels give access to the overhanging part, from which projectiles can be thrown at enemies who have reached the foot of the walls.
Photo Miegeville.

Reconstitution of a throwing machine. The strength of the servants pulling on the rod's short part does not match that produced by a heavy counterweight, but the long part of the rod is prolonged by a device similar to a sling. The sling effect greatly increases the machine's range. Photo Renaud Beffeyte.

Reconstitution of a throwing machine. Machine equipped with a counterweight. A capstan-system helped tower the rod. This type of machine, often called a trebuchet, could throw balls weighing 50 to 80 kgs over 200 metres away, with a precision of only a few metres. Photo Renaud Beffeyte.

THE BIRTH AND EXPANSION OF THE LOWER TOWN

When they returned in 1247, the inhabitants of the destroyed towns that once surrounded the City obtained the right to install themselves on the banks of the Aude. In 1260, a few buildings constructed too near the walls were razed on the orders of the seneschal. In order to avoid this happening again, their inhabitants this time settled on the river's left bank. In 1262, all the inhabitants of Carcassonne living "extra-muros" followed them. The new City developed on flat and open ground. As it was the case for many new towns, the plan that was adopted was simple: a grid pattern, grouped around a central place. Faithful to the memory of the two former boroughs, the inhabitants clustered in two parishes: to the north, Saint-Vincent, to the south, Saint-Michel. The new town was surrounded by a stucco wall, except on the river-side, where the walls were made of stone and used as a dike. As soon as the end of the 8th century, the construction of the present-day Saint-Michel cathedral began. In the beginning of the 14th century, the Saint-Vincent church was raised. In both cases, the choir received a stone vault at it's construction, whereas the only nave, which was very wide, was covered with a structure that rested on the diaphragm arches of the masonry.

The lower town, like the City, had its' own consuls: as an emblem, they chose a lamb carrying the cross. Should one see in this, besides the religious symbol, an allusion to the working of wool which was to become Carcassonne's main activity? This is possible. The exportations of woollen cloth and serge towards Spain were important, and the weavers' guild grew rich enough to occupy, from 1380 onwards, a chapel in the cathedral (Saint-Mathias chapel).

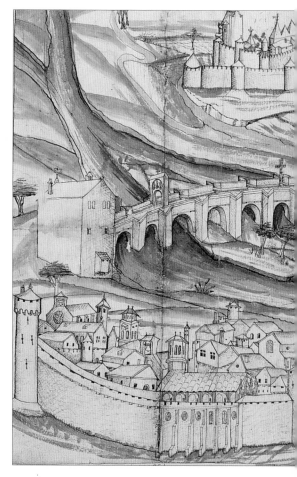

The new town's expansion did not happen without quarrels or calamities: a slight quarrel took place between the township and the butchers, to whom it was forbidden "to kill, within the town walls, any animal for slaughter that could infect the republic". More serious calamities happened, such as the various epidemics, for which the lepers or the Jews were held responsible, the Aude river flood that, in 1377, flooded a part of the town, the 1348 black plague, or the Black Prince's ride, in 1355.

During this particular episode of the Hundred Years' War, the town was taken over by the troops of the Prince of Wales, in spite of the heroic resistance of one of the towns' consuls, Davilla, who was at the head of the few inhabitants who had refused to take refuge in the City. After a due pillage, the town was set ablaze. Almost every wooden or cob house burned down. The town was reconstructed around the church, that had survived the fire, as always according to a grid pattern. Some veritable walls, this time, flanked by small circular towers, surrounded the town. A vestige of these is still visible against the front of the Saint-Michel cathedral. A large ditch preceded the enclosure walls. Despite the stone bridge that connected them at the time, the City and the lower town would, from there on, lead two completely distinct lives.

The lower town and the City in 1462 (NL, ms. VA 17).
In the foreground, the lower town founded under the reign of Saint Louis and rebuilt after
the Black Prince's ride in 1355. The Saint-Michel cathedral rests against the walls.
The river Aude, crossed by the Pont Vieux and divided in several branches, separates the lower town from the City.
National Library, Paris.

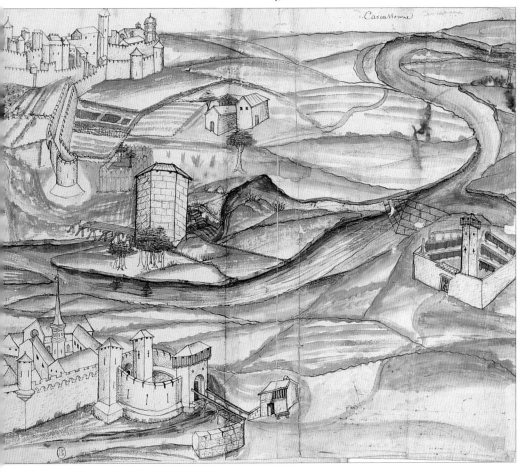

Philippe le Hardi (1270-1285) turns the City into an impregnable fortified town

Under the reigns of Philippe III le Hardi and Philippe IV le Bel, the military vocation of the City was developed.

New, extremely perfected constructions, easily recognisable due to the use of bossing stones, considerably enhanced the inner curtain's defensive value.

The whole southern angle of the walls was rebuilt. Among the newly created strong points, the square Evêque tower stepped over the bailey, thus creating a narrow passage that could easily be controlled. The Saint-Nazaire tower defended the southern City door; its' angled passage made the use of a battering ram very difficult, so the enemy was otherwise forced to advance following to the walls; in this way, he exposed his right flank, which was not protected by a shield, to the low arrow loops of the inner curtain. This curtain, to the south-east, was reshaped similarly to the north walls under the reign of Saint Louis; bossing stone and small Roman masonry alternate in this section.

The will to best defend the eastern front, where the City's main access is, gave birth to the most imposing ensemble. The two enormous towers of the Narbonnaise gate were built in a spur-shape, in order to deflect repeated assaults from battering rams. Their low arrow loops enabled straight shots with crossbows, a weapon whose use had become very frequent. Chains, murder holes, portcullises and heavy doors blocked by thick woden bars followed each other to create a double closing system. A cistern, a salting tub, chimneys and a baker's oven guaranteed the defender's autonomy. On the second floor, the so-called "knights' room" received light, on the City-side, through beautiful gothic windows; it was better conceived as a ceremonial room rather than as a defensive enclave. A slightly complex system of spiral staircases, maybe destined to somewhat disorientate the enemy, granted access to both floors and to the roof timbers.

The nearby Trésau tower owes it's name to the fact that the royal exchequer's (the inland revenue, the *Trésor Public*) offices were located in it. From its' very dark underground level to the parapet that circles the roof, flanked by two watch turrets, one can count four levels resting on vaults or floorboards. As it is the case for all constructions at this time, the niches foreseen for the archers at their shooting stations are equipped with stone benches. From the outside, on the northern flank, one can see the conduit of the perfectly fitted-out latrines, on the second floor. On the City-side, the flat face rises up to a curious Flemish gable, drawn by architects who may have come from the north of France.

Beyond the Trésau tower, the Roman wall, despite being reshaped under Saint Louis, was deemed to be too weak. Razed to the level of the ground, it now appears a little distance back from the homogenous, tall and mighty walls that better defend this particular section, that is made easily accessible by the hill's gentle slope. Further to the north, an abrupt relief enabled the town to make do with the constructions performed under Louis IX.

The importance taken by the relations with the Spanish kingdoms in the politics of Philippe III and his will to affirm the French power in this area probably explain the extent of the works that were performed. In 1272, the king, at the head of a powerful army, stayed in Carcassonne, as he had come to quell a rebellion led by the count of Foix. In 1276, important military preparations preceded an expedition that halted at the feet of the Pyrenean mountains. The purpose of this expedition was to intervene in the succession in Castile.

In 1285 finally, the "Aragon crusade took place". Charles d'Anjou, the king's uncle, chased from his kingdom in Italy by Pierre III of Aragon (the episode of the Sicilian Vespers, March 30th 1282) and pope Martin IV his ally, drove Philippe III to avenge this affront. For this first war that the Capetians led in Europe, outside of the natural limits of France, the army of crusaders was certainly the strongest that a king of France had ever commanded.

Located near the frontier, the City was to be an essential base of operations for this expedition, which in fact turned short. The destruction of the French supply fleet and the black plague which ravaged his troops forced the king to a hasty retreat, just two months after he had crossed the Pyrenean mountains. Ill himself, the king died in Roussillon, on the way back.

The Saint-Nazaire basilisk: the Roman nave, the southern arm of the Gothic transept, the Radulphe chapel and the remains of the canons' cloister.

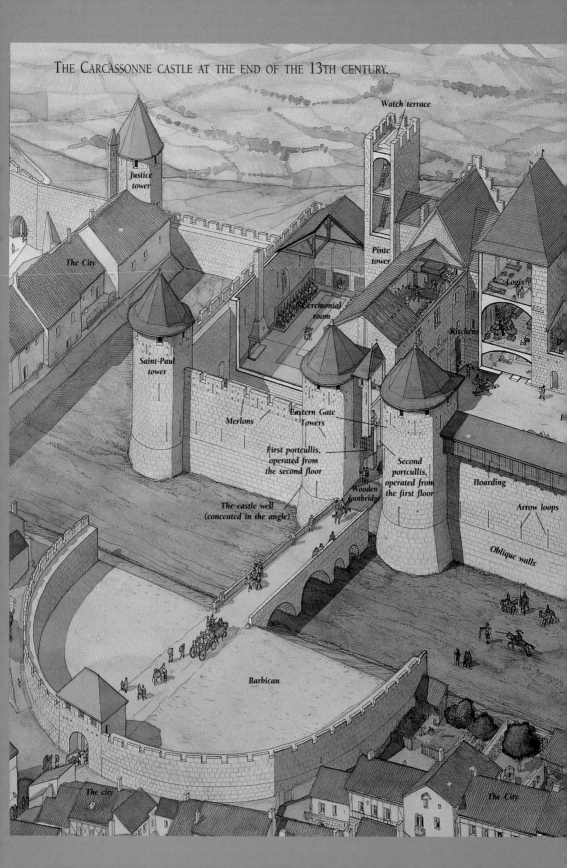

THE CARCASSONNE CASTLE AT THE END OF THE 13TH CENTURY.

Watch terrace

Justice tower

The City

Pinte tower

Logis

Ceremonial room

Kitchens

Saint-Paul tower

Merlons

Eastern Gate Towers

First portcullis, operated from the second floor

Second portcullis, operated from the first floor

Hoarding

The castle well (concealed in the angle)

Wooden footbridge

Arrow loops

Oblique walls

Barbican

The city

The City

The Aude barbican

Mangonnel

Sheltered path,
protected
by two walls

Western entry leading
to the sheltered path

Powder
tower

Chapel
tower

Watchtower

Cellar

Chapel

City walls

Carpenter
(war machines)

Degré
tower

Forge

Saint-Jean's
place market

Stables

Tower
Major

Spiral
staircase

Dry moats

The city

Drawing by Jean-Claude Golvin © Géo, 1993.

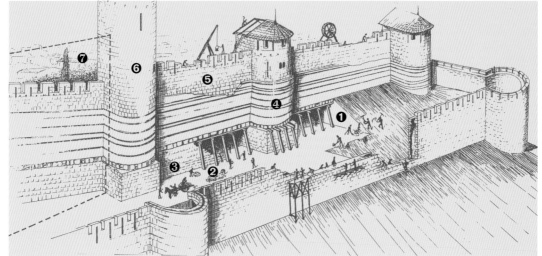

❶
❷
❸
❹
❺
❻
❼

A NEW DEFENSIVE SYSTEM (THE GREAT WORKS OF THE EARLY 8TH CENTURY)

Under the reign of Saint Louis, or more precisely under his mother Blanche de Castille's regency, the City was surrounded with a second curtain. This is a representation of the works on the north-eastern front, near the Narbonnaise gate and the Trésau tower. The space between the two curtains (the bailey), whose profile followed that of the hill, was levelled ❶. The disappearance of the earth talus at the foot of the Gallo-Roman walls revealed their foundations and the ground on which they rested. It would then be easy for the enemy, if he reached the bailey, to dig beneath the masonry, into the soft ground, and to sap the inner curtain. It was therefore necessary to prolong the wall downwards, that is to rebuild it's foundations over a certain depth ❷, so that all it showed the outside was a solid covering of stones ❸.

This rebuilding of the foundations proved to be perilous. Some sections of the walls and towers didn't resist so well when their foundations were unearthed, and lost their balance ❹, there were even a few collapses. The walls were rebuilt, consolidated, and their upper part was even rebuilt and heightened ❺. Nowadays, the Gallo-Roman wall, easily recognisable with its' small masonry and brick wall ties, is mostly caught between the elements that were rebuilt in the 13th century.

Fifty years later, the architects at the service of Philippe le Hardi (1270-1285) would deem this protection to be insufficient, at least to the east, where the hill's slope was gentle and the risks of an attack were therefore greater. They would conceive the immense defences of the Narbonnaise gate and the Trésau tower. An imposing wall made of bossing stones (dotted line - ❼) was to be built ahead of the previously reshaped Roman walls, and would reach the Moulin du Connetable tower ❻.

THE IMPREGNABLE FORTRESS (LATE 13TH CENTURY)

The Narbonnaise gate
❶ salting tub
(food supplies)
❷ cistern
❸ knight's room
❹ entry of the portcullis room
❺ portcullis room

a. machicolation (*)
b. portcullis, operated from the room
c. murder holes
d. machicolation
e. portcullis, operated from the parapet

* the machilocations, like the murder holes, were openings through which all sorts of projectiles could be dropped vertically on the enemy.

*Gargoyle.
Saint-Nazaire
basilisk.*

A wonder of the Midi gothic architecture: the choir and transept of Saint-Nazaire

While the great works were being led to reinforce the inner curtain, the Saint-Nazaire cathedral was deeply modified.

In 1267, the bishop and the chapter announced to the king their intention of gracing the construction with a larger choir and transept.

The diocese's relative poverty and a lack of room inside the City walls were two major obstacles to a total reconstruction. As soon as the works began in 1269, the aim was to try to harmonise the new parts with the Roman nave that was still standing. The transept's vaults therefore rested on circular or square piles, which were blocked with half-columns that were reminiscent of the alternating scheme of Roman pillars. A fairly shallow, seven-sided apse was built proportionately to the nave.

Constructed some forty years earlier, the Parisian Sainte-Chapelle certainly was inspired by the architect of Saint-Nazaire. Twenty-two large statues sculpted in the pillars' stone evoked the twelve apostles, Virgin Mary, Jesus Christ and local saints such as Saint Gimer, Saint Nazaire

Buttress and cornice of the Saint-Nazaire transept's roofing. The sculpted decor is mostly the work of the team under the orders of Viollet-le-Duc (in particular, Perrin, a young Carcassonne sculptor who took part on the construction site from the middle of the 19th century onwards).

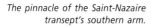

*The pinnacle of the Saint-Nazaire
transept's southern arm.*

or Saint Celse. The apse composes a complete glassware: one window is devoted to the lives of Saint Pierre and Saint Paul, the other to the patrons of the church, Nazaire and Celse. Two great stained glass windows from the 16th century surround a window, in the background, which has kept it's medieval decor (the life of Jesus). The chevet's chapels also welcome glassworks, which are true masterpieces; on the Gospels side, the tree of Jesse, in other words Christ's genealogical tree; on the side of the Epistle, a rare composition, the Tree of life, based on a poetic meditation by Saint Bonaventure (the precepts of life are written in the branches of the tree, the virtues which arise from these are its' fruits). Two magnificent roses order themselves around Virgin Mary who presents her child, to the south, around the Christ in majesty.

As in the Sainte-Chapelle, the walls and vaults were painted, their colours were bright: red or white backgrounds, purple, blue, and yellow for the clothes. Today, one can barely make out the Judgement Day and the Evangelists' symbol on the choir's vault.

It is under bishop Pierre de Rochefort, whose arms (three chess castlings) are affixed on some keys of the vaults and in the centre of the southern rose, that the works were practically finished. The bishop died in 1321; he now rests in the chapel that he had built at the extremity of the north side aisle. His tomb is one of the cathedral's most finely sculpted works. Clumsier and older by about half a century, Guillaume Radulphe's tomb is reminiscent of this Carcasses serf's success, (his name was in fact Razouls) who, under Saint Louis, climbed all the rungs of an ecclesiastic career, right up to the episcopate.

The inhabitants of Carcassonne against the Inquisition

*The twin towers of the Narbonnaise gate.
In the foreground, the Saint-Louis barbican.*

In the gothic transept of Saint-Nazaire, another tombstone, this one more modest and sealed in the wall, deserves equal attention. For at the foot of this epitaph rests Sans Morlane, archdeacon of Carcassonne, who was once convicted by the Inquisition of being a heretic. A true Cathar in his heart and therefore forced to hide his faith, "comprehensive" with the perfects or blatantly hostile to the excesses of the Inquisition, Sans Morlane was to be one of the many notables of Carcassonne to have a brush with the Dominicans. In 1283, he took part in a plot that had a strangely modern flavour. At this time, the Inquisition's registers, which were updated with great care, constituted a dangerous file. Those suspected of being heretics, those who helped, talked with and gave cover to heretics, or even simply failed to denounce them could be arrested at any time. A secret menace therefore threatened most of Carcassonne's inhabitants. A small group of notables, consuls, jurists and others decided to make the fearsome file disappear. The registers were certainly stored in the Justice tower, in the neighbouring house of the Inquisition or in the tower which carried the same name. The conspirers convinced Bernard Lagarrigue, a servant, to steal the documents that were terrorising Carcassonne. A large sum of money was given to him to strengthen his courage but, first contretemps, Lagarrigue admitted not knowing how to read. The chances were he would steal any old document; one found him an accomplice, Bernard Agasse, who worked as a copyist. All was ready. The plot nonetheless fell short, as the Inquisitor had left to Toulouse, taking the key of the archives' storage room.

*The immured people of Carcassonne, oil on canvas by J.-P. Laurens, 1890. A neo-gothic interpretation of the Franciscan monk Bernard Délicieux's struggle against the Inquisition. Immured simply meant imprisoned, since the word "wall", in the middle ages, meant a prison.
Photo: Carcassonne Museum of Fine Arts.*

In the foreground, Christ and the Passion
angel. Sculptures shaped
in the same block of stone as the transept
pillars (late 13th century).
This decor is reminiscent of the decor
in the Parisian Sainte-Chapelle
(where the sculptures may however
be removed from the pillars). In the background, the pillars of the Roman nave
and the side aisle.

The rose window of the north transept,
dedicated to Virgin Mary.

The Saint-Nazaire Cathedral

The vaults of Saint-Nazaire's gothic transept and the northern rose window.
To balance the pressures exerted by vaults that were raised
to the same height, the architects in the early 14th century made
them interdependent, by using iron flyers.

*The Tree of life
(Chapel of the Sainte-Croix,
14th century).
Questionable restoration
of the base.*

*The Tree of Jesse, lower part,
Christ's genealogical tree,
late 13th century.*

Three years later, the climate the Dominicans kept alive in Carcassonne was as heavy as ever. The consuls wrote to Philippe le Bel: " The deplorable result of this oppressive regime are [...]massive emigration out of the kings' domains, depopulation and ruin."

What were the risks? Sometimes, being burned at the stake, but mostly, imprisonment. The prison was located between the river Aude and the City. It was called the "Mur" ["wall"] or the Mure". One could be condemned to the "strict mur", a life sentence of imprisonment during which one was fed only bread and water, or to the "wide mur"; the convicts then lived in a common room, were allowed to take a few steps outside, grow a vegetable garden, have visitors, obtain a furlough and return home when they were ill, or could even be granted a reduction in their sentence if they were leaving a poverty-stricken family behind. These charitable measures frequently gave way to the most cruel methods: in 1325, Guillemette Tournier was burned at the stake in Carcassonne; condemned to the "strict wall", she had confided the dread

Parapet of the inner walls: western front, the so-called gallery of the Inquisition.

she felt for the Church to an informer, a "sheep" who had intentionally been placed in the next cell. Those who were freed were not yet out of the woods: they were made to wear a fabric cloth on their clothes, the sign of infamy, and all their wealth was taken from them. Out of sheer greed, in order to lay their hands on heritages, said the inhabitants of Carcassonne, the inquisitors began taking court actions against the dead. In 1300, they set upon Castel Faure, a notable of the town, who had died twenty two years before.

The Franciscans rose against the Dominicans; their lector, Bernard Delicieux, proved to be a dedicated enemy of the order founded by Saint Dominique. At one time, the royal administration seemed to disown the inquisitors; in Carcassonne, all were exulting; the Dominicans could no longer go to town "without people following them, shouting "coac, coac" the way crows do…". Bernard Delicieux gathered an angry crowd in the cloister of his convent; the Inquisition was shouted down, one ran to free the prisoners and plunder the houses of several informers. The whole of the lower town was ablaze, consul Elie Patrice "who was looked upon as the little king of de Carcassonne" lead the riot. He even began negotiating with the king of Aragon's son, offering to hand the region over to him if he chased the Dominicans away. These events took a turn for the worst; that the people may apply their own laws, that the notables dare express their discontent to the king when he came to visit, that they even thought of finding a better suzerain, was something Philippe le Bel could not tolerate. The lower town was deprived of its' consul and privileges for a while, Elie Patrice and fifteen other bourgeois of Carcassonne were hanged, Bernard Delicieux was condemned by the Roman court to a life sentence in jail.

A mission for the City: to defend the kingdom's south-eastern frontier

Over these years, it was mainly the new town which proved to be uproarious, for the City was no longer the overactive town it had been at the times of the Trencavel. It was now a royal fortified town, and the life that it led was the rather dull life of garrison towns.

Under the Trencavel, as in the first years of the French presence, the small local lords to whom a "borough" (the upkeep of one or two towers) was entrusted as a counterpart for their fief, regularly accomplished their military service under the viscount's orders, then under the orders of the seneschal. But very soon, these feudal lords were to have their ears pulled. As soon as 1268, of 42 feudatories the seneschal called up, only 25 answered his call, and reprimands even had to be renewed for a large number among these.

The inner curtain's parapet where it joins the castles' fortifications.

The decadence of the feudal service caused the institution of sergeants of arms, simple soldiers who were in charge of guarding the City and were under the orders of a constable. Many recruits originated from the north of France, as is shown by the frequent use of first names that were in fashion in these regions: Thierry, Richer, Edouard, Colar, Brion... These soldiers lived at their own expenses in a house in the City. Many married a woman of Carcassonne, and founded a family. Very often, a son took his father's career up; priority over other candidates was actually given to the sergeants of arms' lineage. This post was sought after, not for its' meagre pay, but for the prestige, the various benefits in kind and the fiscal

The inner curtain's parapet; southern front, the Moulin du Midi tower.

exemptions. As soon as the early 16th century, sergeants had their own association : "the brotherhood of Saint-Louis". How many were they? What was their regular strength? On a payment roll dated 1260, one could only find some sixty names for a daily salary of 8 deniers (a little less than a workman in the building trade earned). But some feudal lords were still requested to constitute an complementary military force. A 14th century text alludes to the City's 200 sergeants, who were paid a daily salary of 12 deniers. These

The Justice tower and the Pinte tower (counts' castle).

figures are plausible. Towards the end of the Middle Ages, the garrison was apparently reduced by half and counted but 109 men. Strictly speaking, one should of course add to the count of the military all the technicians, craftsmen and "engineers" who were at the service of the army.

In times of peace, the sergeants guarded the entries of the town in rotations. The night guard had 34 of them on duty every evening. Some took place on the curtains at fixed posts, others set themselves up in the guardroom of the Narbonnaise gate; others, finally, went on their rounds in the bailey (8 rounds in summer, 12 in winter when nights were longer). From the top of the walls, their comrades were to answer their calls and report any incident. All were to show up in the regulation uniform, wearing a "bassinet" (an iron skullcap)over their "cappa magna" (a chain mail hood), armed with their crossbows, and their sword by their side. Discipline was strict and absences were punished by heavy fines.

This was due to the fact that the City was one of the main fortified towns, the guardian of the border between France and Spain. The Roussillon was not French land, the limit between the kingdom of France and the kingdom of Aragon was drawn accordingly to a line of Pyrenean crests that more or less matched the present-day limit between the actual Aude and Pyrenees-Orientales departments. On this line, Louis IX had many eyries enlarged and enhanced: Puylaurens, Peyrepertuse, Queribus, Termes, Aguilar now proudly testified to the royal might. Signalling towers, atop which fires were lit, echoed any alert in the distance to Carcassonne. The City was the impassable defensive lock that was to immediately halt any invasion, and enable counter-attacks.

The garrison possessed a considerable arsenal. An inventory drawn up in 1298 concerning the equipment stored by the Charpentiere tower, near the castle, mentions various war machines: trebuchets, mangonnels, balistas, hooks, ropes, counterweights, siege equipment, (scaffoldings, ladders, stakes and pickaxes for sapping and counter-sapping), building equipment, necessary objects for jousts (pavilions, masts, platforms, stockades, tents...), a large number of containers (barrels, vats), whetstones...

From the City were dispatched ammunitions or equipment for various military campaigns. In 1234, 900 crossbows of various types and 250 crates of specific bolts were sent to Agen upon the king's demand. In 1345, the City provided three dozen siege slings with their equipment. The stock of weaponry was unceasingly renewed and modernised. In 1412, "a large metallic bombard" created a sensation upon its' arrival in Carcassonne.

The decline

By the end of the 15th century, powder artillery had replaced the ancient siege machines. One century later, the power of the canons was so great, that only ramparted walls, i.e. walls protected by thick earth embankments, could resist their shots. Not adapted to these new weapons, the City soon became a technically outdated construction. Its' strategic value, however, remained untouched, as the Spanish border lay nearby. One hundred and ten "morte-payes" ("dead pays", people exempted of paying tax) ensured a guard service in order to prevent the place from falling by surprise in the enemy's hands. They were the inheritors of the sergeants of arms who were installed after the annexation to the royal domain. The office was transmissible, the wages (40 "sous" [shillings] per month) in the beginning of the 17th century (a weaver, at the same epoch, earned four or five times more) and the supply of a certain quantity of salt were not enough for a family to live on. But the service was not daily, and became less constraining. Most of the "morte-payes" therefore had another job; they worked as wool carders, hotel-keepers, clerks, embroiders, dressmakers, farmers, school teachers, cloth-workers, weavers, builders, locksmiths, bailiffs, merchants… Two yearly reviews for Saint-Jean-Baptiste's day and for Saint-Louis' day gave them the opportunity of going, with great pomp, to the small Saint-Sernin church, which has now disappeared (a gothic window in a Gallo-Roman tower near the Narbonnaise gate is all that remains of it). Before attending the "masses and vespers", the proud guardians of the City fired salvoes with their arquebuses… not always with great care, for in 1619 "Barthélémie, wife of Pierre Albouy" who was admiring the procession from her balcony "suffered a wound at her left buttock", "the said wound occurred fortuitously and unexpectedly, with no malice or deliberate act involved … ".

The religious conflicts in the 16th century opposed the fiercely catholic City to the protestant armies. In these wars of skirmishes and ambushes, that were waged with very restrained means, the walls once again perfectly played their role. In any case, they inspired the little king Charles IX, who was visiting Carcassonne with his mother Catherine de Médicis in January 1565: "Snow fell in such great profusion […] that the young king took pleasure in building a fortress of snow that was defended by those of his house and attacked by those of the upper- and lower towns."

In 1659, the Pyrenean peace marked the definitive annexation of the Roussillon to the kingdom. The border between France and Spain moved further away from Carcassonne. Already technically out of date, the place lost most of its' strategic interest. The decline of the Spanish might, the long-lived peace which reigned on this frontier finally took all military value away from the City.

The Vade and Balthazar towers
before their restoration.
Photo Departmental Archives of the Aude.

CARCASSONNE, A LARGE INDUSTRIAL TOWN

This statement may be surprising when applied to a town that now mainly lives off its' administrative functions and local trade. The economic situation in the 18th century was totally different: Carcassonne was then one of the kingdom's first fabric production centres. The town was "in fact just a factory for all kinds of cloths", stated the intendant of the province in 1698, "all its' inhabitants are occupied with this, some spinning, some carding and all other activities…". One century later, Arthur Young, in his travel diary, mentioned Carcassonne as "one of the most considerable factory sites in France". An ancient activity, that existed as early as in the Middle Ages, the production of woollen fabrics developed in the 17th century and hit its' peak in the first half of the 18th century.

Brought from the Montagne Noire and the Corbières, but also widely imported from Spain, the wool was washed, sorted, carded, spun, fulled, matted, dyed, readied in a number of workshops or in a few large factories. As it was customary under the Ancien Régime, part of the production was also performed in the countryside, since the manufacturers-merchants of Carcassonne had developed a complete network of merchants of Carcassonne had developed a complete network of home-workers.

The greater part of the production was exported, via Marseille, towards the Middle East, to the large ports where Europeans had established trading posts: Constantinople, Smyrn, Beyrut, Alep, Cyprus, Alexandria. The Carcassonne woollen cloths now competed with the English production, right to the names of the fabrics themselves: the "londrins", or cloths made "the London way". A key element of Colbertism, of the "commercial war" the way Colbert conceived it, the quality requirements are general, and especially effective in the royal factories. Private companies boasting this title accepted very rigorous controls, but were in return granted subventions for exportation. The Trivalle factory, located between the City and the lower town, produced, in 1740, 132 bundles of woollen cloth, but large manufacturers like Antoine Rolland or Pierre Cavailhes attained the same production level, and the total length of the woollen cloth produced yearly by Carcassonne and its' region could be counted in hundreds of kilometres (for a standard width of 1,40 m).

Renowned for their solidity, their range of colours and the resistance of their dyes, these woollen cloths sold very well, so wide open was the Middle East market, which was capable of accepting a production that never ceased to increase during the beginning of the 18th century.

Making the most of this prosperity, the lower town experienced, right through the 18th century, many "embellishments": from 1751 to 1761, Jean-François Cavailhes, a rich, noble cloth manufacturer, had a luxurious private mansion built. This building, which was later bought by the Rolland family and is since then known as the "hôtel de Rolland", now is the town hall of Carcassonne. In 1771, the Herbes place (the present-day Carneau place) received a monumental fountain to the glory of Neptune, a fountain that, more prosaically, was the crowning achievement of the water conveyance works the town carried out. Street lighting and paving, the construction of the covered markets, the filling of the ditches, which were transformed into sheltered promenades under the impulse of Monseigneur de Bezons, the construction of a monumental door in the shape of the Arc de Triomphe at the south entry of the City (the Jacobins portal), all was done to make forget about the old town, founded under Saint Louis, and rebuilt after the devastating conquest led by the Black Prince in 1355. Only the City's grid pattern is now reminiscent of the original walled town.

The canal du Midi, the lower town with its' two main churches, Saint-Vincent and Saint-Michel. Avenues have replaced the ditch and walls. In the distance, the river Aude and the City. View from an air balloon. Lithography by Alfred Guesdon, ca. 1848. Toulouse, Paul-Dupuy Museum.

Active and prosperous, the lower town attracted distinguished people to it. Many magistrates and officers lived there. In the middle of the 17th century, after a long-lasting quarrel between the inhabitants of the City and those of the market towns, the seat of the presidia was definitely transferred to the lower town. One hundred years later, the bishop Monseigneur de Bezons had a vast episcopal palace constructed, surrounded by very beautiful gardens (the present-day prefecture). Was living in the City a penance? Monseigneur, on all accounts, only resided there during Lent.

A progressively saturated market, the renewal of the English competition, a decline in quality which was meant to compensate falling prices, the isolation of France during the revolutionary wars and under the Empire dealt as many lethal blows to a mono-industry that never found new markets or changed activities. Under the Restoration, the woollen cloth-making activities took off again, becoming increasingly mechanised, but never rose to the level they had attained in the past century. The Carcassonne capitals were from there on sooner invested in vines and the production of equipment destined to viticulture. Weaving, and especially spinning, which embodied the larger part of the textile activities, survived only thanks to the trade workers' low salaries.

The Narbonnaise gate passage.

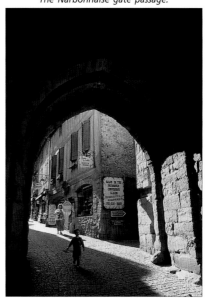

One could now count the City among the most poverty-stricken districts. This is a statement by Doctor Villermé, in the great public survey he published in 1840 on "the mental and physical state of workers" in France: "It would be hard to imagine, had one not seen it, the poverty that reigns in this last district of Carcassonne, where many weavers and other workers among the factory's poorest are gathered. One can only see narrow, winding streets, badly constructed houses that are filthy indoors, ground floors that are mostly dark and damp, housings that are badly furnished, too small for

The Canal du Midi

To create his "canal of the two seas" (1666-1681), Paul Riquet had to solve two essential problems:

– the first was the flooding of the canal. This was performed at the level of the sill of Naurouze. It was already known that this modest pass drew a dividing line: to the west, the waters run towards the Atlantic, to the East, towards the Mediterranean. It is at this dividing point that the canal is supplied in water. The Montagne Noire overlooks, to the south, the sill of Naurouze, and Riquet, who owned an estate there discovered a network of streams which he diverted to form some reservoirs (Saint-Ferreol lake, Lampy lake). From there, the water flowed downhill to Naurouze in a channel he had dug.

– the second was the financing of a considerable construction site, over 200 km long, which employed 10 000 people and required technical wizardry, that was astonishing at that time, to be achieved (a bridge on which the canal crossed over a river, the Répudre, the Enserune tunnel...). Riquet operated a " set-up " by associating private capitals (all his fortune, and part of financier Reich de Pennautier's too...), State aids - since Colbert approved the project, the royal treasury participated to about one third -, funds from the province, the Languedoc estates, thanks to a special tax, contributed to approximately one half of the total cost, and funds from the town that the canal would serve.

The Carcassonne town council was reluctant to pay. Small boats could still follow the Aude downstream to transport packets of woollen cloth to the sea, where they would then reach Marseille before being sent to the Middle East. One century later, the situation had changed. The Eastern market was mostly closed to foreign products, and one began looking for opportunities within the kingdom. Besides, after the great winter of 1709, the Languedoc vineyards, that had suffered less damage than their northern rivals, began to supply Paris. A Carcassonne-Toulouse waterway connection seemed increasingly imperative. This is probably why the population of Carcassonne required and obtained that the canal be diverted. In 1810, the harbour was opened on the northern flank of the lower town.

their own inhabitants, who have in turn almost become destitute." The castle accommodated a few civil servants and injured soldiers. Like the Parisian Bastille, it was used as a royal prison. On the dawn of the Revolution, the prisoners locked upon "lettres de cachet" ranged from a womanising ecclesiastic to an ungrateful son, who was imprisoned on his parents' demand: he continuously insulted his mother and stole his respectable family's money, which he squandered in taverns.

The neglected towers of both sets of walls saw their roofs slowly fall into decay. The bailey, in sections where it was wide enough, simply became a street. Over a hundred houses were built, either against the inner walls or facing them. The battlements' stones were pulled free and reused by those who would take them. Some towers became storerooms, workshops or cellars where the wine could be kept cool. In the Age of the Enlightenment as under the Revolution, the administration didn't care much for this souvenir of the cursed Middle Ages. In November 1793, a bonfire was lit using the City's rich collection of archives. In the following years, nothing was done to prevent this downgraded fortification from becoming a simple stone quarry. The solidity of the walls alone hindered these more or less clandestine pillages. In 1850 finally, a decree handed the whole fortifications over to the demolition crews' pickaxes.

THE HERITAGE: FROM RECOGNITION TO RENOWN

The restorations, the renewal

A Carcassonne scholar, Jean-Pierre Cross-Mayrevieille, would save the towers and walls from their impending destruction. With the help of his action and of those of Merimee and Viollet-le-Duc, the fortifications were placed under the authority of what was then called "the administration of fine arts". Since 1844, Viollet-le-Duc was working on the restoration of the Saint-Nazaire church. Fascinated by this monument, he observed, sketched, and watched over the works: "I am here the whole blessed day, among a whole lot of old women who come to confession and have no qualms about giving me their fleas...", he wrote to his wife. Used to store fodder during the Revolution, returned to the Cult but deprived of its' title of cathedral (which was given to Saint-Michel in 1803), the construction was in a pitiful state. All of the great architect's skill was needed to avoid a total ruin.

The City then slightly came back to life: "I created, wrote Viollet-le-Duc, a construction site with workers mostly chosen among the locals... Here, I have builders, stone-cutters, blacksmiths, carpenters, sculptors, all men are used to difficult tasks, all work near their homes, all are under my guidance." Some of these Carcassonne workers, such as the sculptor Perrin or the architect Cals, were truly talented. From 1855 onwards, the restoration of the fortifications began. In 1879, at the death of Viollet-le-Duc, they were far from finished. His pupil, Boeswillwald, then the architect Nodet would complete the master's enterprise.

Often criticised, Viollet-le-Duc's work has been judged with far less severity over the past few years. The romantic climate of the middle of 19th century and the enthusiastic faith the first archaeologists placed in their science of course marked the restorations of Saint-Nazaire, as well as those of the fortress; the finished style (not a single merlon is missing on the battlements), a stressed didactical will (reconstitution of the hoarding), aesthetically successful but somewhat questionable reconstructions (the castle's western face) deprive the monument of any absolute authenticity. Viollet-le-Duc however used his knowledge to the utmost, and attained marvellous comprehension of the medieval military architecture. The work of Viollet-le-Duc has today entered history. In the years 1950-1960, some previous restorations were "corrected": convex tiles, closer in their use to the Roman equipment, replaced the slates on the roofing of the Bas-Empire towers, without it actually being asserted that these towers originally were covered.

For the Trésau tower and the Narbonnaise gate, flat tiles were substituted to slate tiles. This was not in order to quieten those inhabitants of Carcassonne who were radically opposed to the use of slate, which was "so untypical of the South", but rather to leave the mark of the royal architects of the end of the 13th and beginning of the 14th centuries. These, as some documents from the archives suggest, maybe used this material, with which they were familiar. Nowadays, when an intervention is necessary, restorations are performed exactly as the building had been constructed, thus conserving the personal touch of Viollet-le-Duc, which has become a typical element of the City's heritage. The restored parts represent less than 30 % of the monument. Roofs, frameworks and battlements represent, with the consolidation of some vaults, the major part of these restorations.

THE RESTORATIONS OF VIOLLET-LE-DUC

These watercolour paintings by Viollet-le-Duc
are not restoration projects
but studies destined to graphically render the
state of the City at the end of the 13th century.

Photos by Miegeville.

The Vade tower, crowned with hoarding.

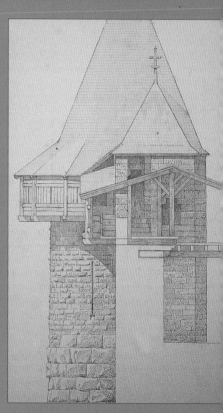

Side view of the Trauquet tower and rampart
walk, crowned with hoarding.

Eastern gate of the counts' castle.

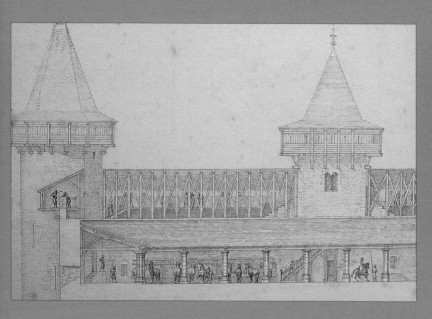

Inner face of the counts'
castle's curtain.
Stables on the ground level.
Hoarding galleries at the
level of the rampart walk.

The Trauquet tower,
front view.

The Narbonnaise gate.

Some famous inhabitants of Carcassonne

The appeal of the last victims of The reign of Terror in the Saint-Lazare prison. 7-9th Thermidor 1794, by Charles Louis Muller. Versailles and Trianon Museum. © RMN.

André Chenier (1762-1794)

The son of a "beautiful Greek woman" and of a cloth-maker and merchant of Carcassonne who represented the French interests in Constantinople, André Chenier was born in this town, but spent part of his childhood in Carcassonne. He then frequented the Parisian salons, travelled, was enthusiastic about the ideals of 1789 and the conquering of the Rights of Man, but was very critical with the excesses of the Jacobins. Imprisoned under the Reign of Terror, he was guillotined on Thermidor 7th, year II, in spite of the cautious efforts his brother Marie-Joseph (the author of the lyrics to the *"Chant du départ"*) made to save him. A great admirer of ancient Greece and a man committed to his times who searched to reconcile sincere inspiration with formal beauty, Chenier, whose works were first published in 1819, had a strong influence on the poets of the 19th century.

Fabre d'Eglantine (1750-1794)

Philippe Fabre was also born of a family of cloth-makers and merchants. On the pretext that he had received the "gold eglantine" at the Toulouse Floral Games (a literary contest, in which the prize-winners received a flower made of gold or silver), he spread his name as Fabre d'Eglantine. An itinerant comedian and drama writer, he obtained very unequal successes. "Il pleut, il pleut bergère", the romance of an operetta he composed in Maestricht in 1780 still remains in everybody's mind. A friend of Danton and of Camille Desmoulins, his political role under the Revolution nonetheless remained in the background, and his attitude was changing, to say the least. Some of his writings sometimes were as violent as those of Marat, but his poet's mind resurfaced when he gave their names to the months of the revolutionary calendar. Wrongly accused by Robespierre of being corrupt, he was guillotined on Germinal 16th, year II.

Portrait of Fabre d'Eglantine, beginning of the 18th century. Versailles and Trianon museum. © RMN.

Barbès (1809-1870)

Armand Barbès was born in Pointe-à-Pitre, where his father worked as a doctor in the military. In 1815, his father retired to Carcassonne where he came from and lived the life of a rich landowner. The childhood and adolescence of Armand Barbes in Carcassonne were happy and rather indolent, and contrast with the restless life of republican conspiracies he then led. Under the July Monarchy, he was arrested several times when he was supposed to be studying law in Paris.

At first a simple Republican, his thoughts then evolved towards social issues, but Barbès was more a brave and generous man of action than a theoretician. Elected to be the deputy for the Aude in the Constituent Assembly after the 1848 revolution, he fought the conservative drift of the 2nd republic and once again ended up in prison. Freed in 1854 by Napoleon III, he refused the amnesty he was offered and voluntarily went into exile to the Netherlands, where he died only a few weeks before the fall of the second Empire. Nicknamed "the Bayard of Democracy" by his friends, Barbès remains a dear memory, as one of Carcassonne's most implied defenders of freedom, and it is in front of his statue that the opponents of the Vichy government demonstrated their refusal to collaborate in 1941 and 1942.

Joë Bousquet (1897-1950)

In May 1918, a serious wound of war lost Joë Bousquet the use of his legs. From there on, he would no longer leave the "bedroom with closed shutters" of his house in Carcassonne. The title of his most famous work: "Traduit du silence", accounts for the subtle art with which he expresses the mysterious authenticity of an inner life.

This quest for knowledge and his demanding poetry did however not make Bousquet a solitary man. Attentive to his town, he described its' society with sharp humour in "Le médisant par bonté" (1945). Above all, as soon as 1924, he committed himself alongside the surrealists, became a friend of Eluard, of Breton, of Max Ernst... Jean Paulhan, Gide, Valéry visited him and mixed in with his Carcassonne friends, the poet François-Paul Alibert, the philosopher Louis-Claude Esteve, the author René Nelli.

Photograph of Joë Bousquet, taken between 1944 and 1946 by Gabriel Sarraute. © Journal "Joë Bousquet et son Temps" (1997) (Maison Joë Bousquet - 53 rue de Verdun, Carcassonne.)

Under the occupation, his house gave shelter to intellectuals and artists who were threatened by the nazis, and today still is a Mecca for the spirit, that one should not fail to visit.

At the beginning of this century, the City, which had become a fabulous museum of medieval architecture, was a place in which the international high society enjoyed stopping between a vacation in Biarritz and another on the Côte d'Azur. The lower town developed as the prefecture of a department whose wine production has become its' main wealth. In May 1907, as Languedoc was experiencing a crisis due to overproduction, which gave birth to a burst of strong discontent, Carcassonne welcomed one of the most important demonstrations of wine growers that the poor wine sales caused.

Nowadays

From the 20th century onwards, the development of tourism gave Carcassonne, a medium-sized provincial town in the heart of a department where life is pleasant, a new vocation. The City, which welcomed a little under 10 000 visitors in the beginning of the century, presently welcomes about two million tourists every year. An intriguing challenge for a monument whose first role was to repel any intrusions; the inhabitants of Carcassonne take it up with ingenuity and good spirit.

But over all, the City is no more a prestigious, isolated monument, it is the heart of an ambitious plan for tourists that the people of the Aude have set up to develop their region: the charms of the lower town, the major Catharic places, the vertiginous castles of the Corbières and of the Montagne Noire, Romanic chapels, Cistercian abbeys, art, archaeology or ethnology museums, lakes and beaches, walks during which one may discover an infinite range of landscapes ...

The castle, the towers, the walls, the bailey belong to the State, the rest is part of the town's domain. Conscious as they are of the value their heritage possesses, more and more inhabitants "rehabilitate" their houses but also, very frequently, open a shop in them.

May the crowds not discourage the lovers of the past. Even at the peak of the tourist season, before ten in the morning, after six in the afternoon, the City is once again calm. It is at this moment that the light is the most beautiful. This is the time to walk up the Cross-Mayrevieille street, to discover the great and small wells (Grand et Petit Puits), to saunter around the streets and linger on the Marcou place before walking through the bailey in search of the Grand Canissou tower, of the Aude gate, of the Cremade barbican or the Avar postern.

GLOSSARY

Bailey: the space between two enclosures.

Barbican: advanced fortification which protects an entry.

Bartizan: watchtower.

Bastion: a turret placed at an angle of a construction.

Battlement: open part of the parapet which protects the rampart walk, and from which one can shoot and survey the land outside.

Brattice: overhang usually built over a door and pierced with an murder hole.

Curtain: wall section between two tours.

Lining: fortified enclosure around a dungeon.

Flanking: the possibility to shoot not only face on, but also to the side thanks to a overhang of the construction. Towers are flanking works.

Hoarding: wooden gallery placed before the battlements and that hangs over the base of the walls. Equipped with holes in its' floor, the hoarding enabled the defenders to reach then enemy who had reached the base of the walls.

Machicolation: opening through which projectiles were thrown towards the ground. By extension, stone galleries built according to the principles of the hoarding in castles at the end of the Middle Ages.

Masonry: the manner in which the stones of a wall are cut and laid out. Masonry may be characterised by it's dimensions (small, medium, or large masonry, cyclopean masonry in the case of very large blocks), by it's surface (bossing masonry: stones of which only the edges have been levelled and whose centre part projects, like a bossing), or by it's disposition (regular, irregular, fish-boned...).

Merlon: the filled parts of the crenelations.

Moat: ditch below the walls. Dry moats are ditches without water.

Murder hole: opening in a vault, through which projectiles were thrown.

Sheltered path: path sheltered by two lateral walls, thanks to which one could walk along it under cover.

Tapering: the slope of a wall that widens at it's base.

The western front by night.

Between the Saint-Nazaire basilisk and the southern angle of the fortifications: the theatre.

A medieval show in the southern bailey, in the month of August.

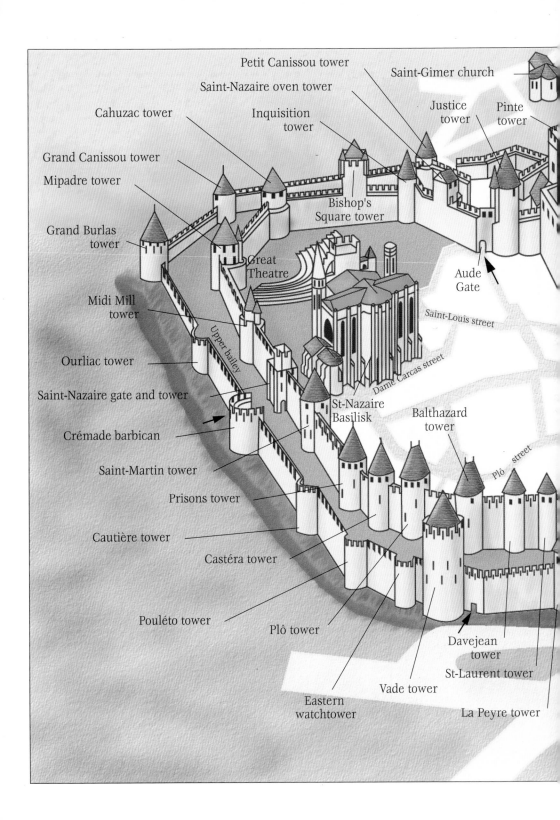

Petit Canissou tower

Saint-Nazaire oven tower

Saint-Gimer church

Cahuzac tower

Inquisition tower

Justice tower

Pinte tower

Grand Canissou tower

Mipadre tower

Bishop's Square tower

Grand Burlas tower

Great Theatre

Aude Gate

Midi Mill tower

Saint-Louis street

Upper bailey

Dame Carcas street

Ourliac tower

Saint-Nazaire gate and tower

St-Nazaire Basilisk

Balthazard tower

Crémade barbican

Plô street

Saint-Martin tower

Prisons tower

Cautière tower

Castéra tower

Pouléto tower

Plô tower

Davejean tower

St-Laurent tower

Eastern watchtower

Vade tower

La Peyre tower

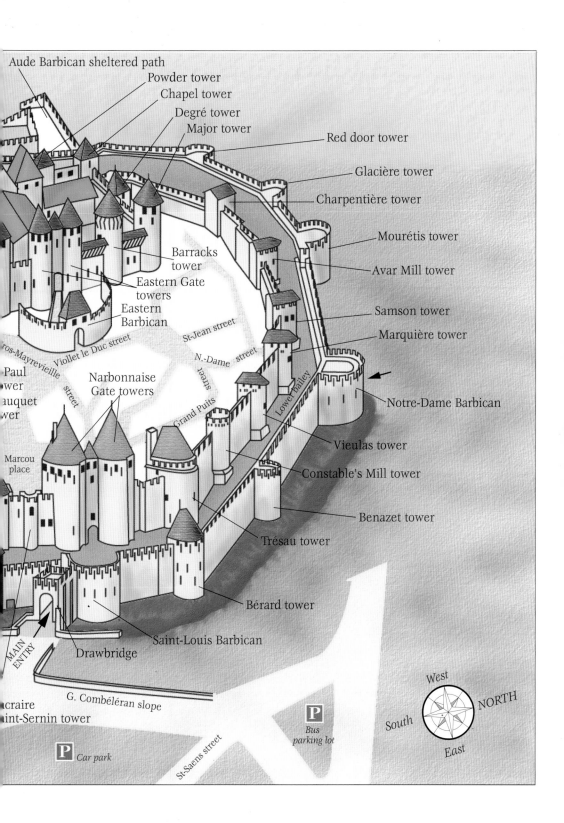

Aude Barbican sheltered path
Powder tower
Chapel tower
Degré tower
Major tower
Red door tower
Glacière tower
Charpentière tower
Mourétis tower
Barracks tower
Avar Mill tower
Eastern Gate towers
Eastern Barbican
Samson tower
Marquière tower
ros-Mayrevieille street
Viollet le Duc street
St-Jean street
N.-Dame street
Paul wer
auquet wer
Narbonnaise Gate towers
Lower bailey
Notre-Dame Barbican
Marcou place
Grand Puits street
Vieulas tower
Constable's Mill tower
Benazet tower
Trésau tower
Bérard tower
Saint-Louis Barbican
Drawbridge
MAIN ENTRY
craire
int-Sernin tower
G. Combéléran slope
West
NORTH
South
East
P Bus parking lot
P Car park
St-Saens street

63

PRACTICAL INFORMATION

The City
Free visits:
The bailey: a one-and-a-half kilometre walk between the walls.
The Saint-Nazaire basilisk
The City's streets and places
Some towers (Narbonnaise towers, Trésau tower...): branch of the Tourist Office, welcome-point
of the Historical monuments and sites office, promotion of regional wines.
Pay-to-enter sites:
The count's castle, a circuit on the outer walls' curtains
Between the City and the lower town, by taking the Trivalle street:
Rue Trivalle :
n° 25, house of the Montmorency (16th century)
n° 64, house of Pierre Pelletier (beginning of the 17th century, very archaistic)
n° 3, entry piece of the Trivalle royal factory

The Pont Vieux (14th century).

In the lower town
Carnot place
House of the memories (53, Verdun street): Catharic studies centre, permanent exposition devoted to Joë Bousquet and his friends, Ethnology research group
Museum of Fine Arts (1, Verdun street)
Rolland hall (32, Aime-Ramon street)
Saint-Michel cathedral and its' treasure
The Saint-Vincent church
Near the railway station, the port of the canal du Midi and to the east, the walk along the towpath

Yearly happenings

In July, the City festival (theatre, music, ballet dances).
On July 14th, exceptional fireworks and the " blazing City ".
In August, the "Medieval days": nocturnal show. Animations in the streets, jousts in the bailey...

BIBLIOGRAPHY

Bousquet (Joë) *Le médisant par bonté* - Reprint: L'imaginaire/Gallimard, 1980
Brenon (Anne) *Les cathares, pauvres du Christ ou Apôtres de Satan* - Découvertes-Gallimard, 1997
Gougaud (Henri) (adapted by...) *La chanson de la croisade albigeoise* - Le Livre de poche "Lettres gothiques", 1989

© 1999 Édilarge SA – Éditions Ouest-France, Rennes
This book was printed by Mame Imprimeurs in Tours (37) – n° 02062126
ISBN 2 7373 2497 1 – Registration of copyright : Mars 1999 – Editor N° 3885 03.02.07.02